Re: American Dream

Six Urban Housing Prototypes from Los Angeles

Princeton Architectural Press

Re: American Dream is based on an exhibit that took place at the Municipal Art Gallery, Los Angeles. It was organized by Ed Leffingwell, former director of the gallery, with the cooperation of the Southern California Institute of Architecture. Funding was provided by a grant from the Graham Foundation for Advanced Studies in the Fine Arts.

First published in the United States by Princeton Architectural Press and Los Angeles Municipal Art Gallery Associates.

library of congress cataloging-in-publication data

Re: American dream : six urban housing prototypes for Los Angeles.
p. cm.
Includes bibliographical references.
ISBN 1-56898-027-2
1. Architecture. Domestic-California-Los Angeles.
2. Architecture. Modern-20th century-California-Los Angeles. 3. Housing.
Single family-California-Los Angeles.
NA7238.L6R4 1995
728'.37'0979794-dc20
94-17461
CIP

# With Re: American Dream, a group of innovative Los Angeles-based architects redefine what constitutes property and ownership, and reconsider notions of housing, neighborhood, and the significance of home.

This project has been funded in part by the Graham Foundation for Advanced Studies in the Fine Arts, as well as by the Southern California Institute of Architecture, and we are grateful for their commitment and support.

As a design study, exhibition, and publication, this project was initiated and proposed to the Los Angeles Municipal Art Gallery by architect Roger Sherman and his colleagues Janek Bielski, Ron Golan, Eric Kahn, Russell N. Thomsen, Danelle Guthrie, Tom Buresh, Steve Johnson, James Favaro, and Mary-Ann Ray. The participants set parameters for their research and developed theoretical solutions to specific geographic, topographic, and socio-economic circumstances, eventually meeting monthly to debate their individual conclusions and to formulate their presentations. We are grateful for their initiative and perseverance.

Designers Whitney Lowe and Lorraine Wild worked with the architects to develop elements of a handsome and cohesive exhibition format, consistent with the intended publication design. Credit also goes to Tom Bonner for the architectural photography included here. We are indebted to Gallery Curator Noel Korten for serving as staff liaison for all aspects of the exhibition, to Chief Preparator Michael Miller for directing the exhibit's fabrication and installation, and to Education Director Carla Fantozzi for coordinating a symposium convening private citizens and urban planners to consider and reformulate their respective dreams.

We gratefully acknowledge the ongoing support of the City of Los Angeles Cultural Affairs Department, of which the gallery is a facility, the leadership and financial commitment of the directors of the gallery at Barnsdall Art Park, and the Los Angeles Municipal Art Gallery Associates. We are pleased to collaborate with the participating architects and Princeton Architectural Press in the co-publication of this document.

—Edward Leffingwell

Former Director

Los Angeles Municipal Art Gallery

**The ideas for this book** and for the collection of essays, projects, and analytical drawings contained within it were born five years ago, when I first arrived in Los Angeles from New York City and went about looking for a place to live. The experience engendered a realization of the need to bring greater critical awareness to the suburban vision as embodied in the single-family detached house, perhaps the most significant American contribution to the history of the design of the built landscape. No less than the skyscraper serves as the preeminent icon of American commercial aspiration, the suburban tract home emblemizes par excellence the American domestic vision rooted in the Jeffersonian agrarian ideal that "as few as possible shall be without a small portion of land."

In Los Angeles, however, the pressures of a changing socio-economic climate are causing this dream to rapidly become an anachronism. The unavoidable consequence of the city's increasing population has been the per capita reduction of available land and, concomitantly, the increase in the cost of owning property. Inexorably, the dream of home ownership is slipping out of the reach of an increasing percentage of the population. Only by challenging current zoning practices, questioning customary relationships between property and ownership, and attending to the changing program of the single-family home itself, as the proposals which appear herein do, can we as architects and urbanists succeed in stimulating first the discourse and thereby the action necessary to insure that the American Dream remains alive, if perhaps in an alternative form. As such, this publication should be viewed as more an anthology of analytical and speculative ventures than a set of conclusive or authoritative solutions to this problem.

**Toward this end,** I wish to thank those who participated in the symposium held during the exhibition for their valuable comments and enthusiastic call for a response to and realization of the ideas represented in the projects: Dana Cuff, Emily Gable, Craig Hodgetts, Eugene Kupper, Stefanos Polyzoides, Michael Rotondi, Edward Soja, Councilman Michael Woo, and especially Aaron Betsky, who provided us with early guidance.

**I wish to extend** our gratitude to the Graham Foundation for Advanced Studies in the Fine Arts for their generous grant, without which the "Dream" never would have been realized. Michael Rotondi and Richard Weinstein also deserve thanks for their generous support, and for allowing SCI-Arc and UCLA to serve as venues in which to openly discuss the issues raised by the show within the Los Angeles community-at-large. Kevin Lippert also deserves thanks for his unflagging interest, patience, and receptivity to our ideas for the catalog. And lastly, I speak for the entire group of architects whose work is exhibited on the following pages when I acknowledge an enormous debt of gratitude to all of those students, too numerous to name here, who enthusiastically dedicated a substantial portion of their summer break working for little compensation when they might well have been doing something else. Without their contribution, this work would be in every respect less complete.

Richard Weinstein

The issues which arise when one considers the single-family
house in the context of Los Angeles seem once-removed from the con-
troversies currently at the center of international architectural debate.
The honorable tradition of concern for housing, once an important criteria by which we measured our architects, has been diminished,
partly because government funding for housing has collapsed but perhaps more importantly because architects have become more
interested in the house than in housing.

But there is a further explanation: since the partial eclipse of
modernism those architects excited by the postmodern have turned
their backs on the social concerns of modernism and embraced establishment patrons; those architects excited by European critical theory
have adopted strategies related to conceptual art, using their work to
express critical social concerns while avoiding what they saw as com-
promising associations. In this way the conscience of modern
architecture went underground to reemerge in radical form, though
with little direct impact on the world as it is.

Circumstances, however, are changing and there is increasing
movement toward direct intervention. This welcome trend, painfully
accelerated by the recent civil disturbances in Los Angeles, actively
engages the social implications of the building arts.

The exhibition upon which this book is based repositions housing
as central to architectual discourse. Despite all the practical issues
which constrain their free expression, these gifted architects are never-
theless engaging the problem in the Los Angeles setting where it is
most urgent. While no single proposal can master the subject, each reveals something of significance and raises issues of both ideology and
design which must be addressed. Out of what we value and what we
may learn to discard, the effort to assemble a new attitude toward
housing can begin.

# Order in the House

Sylvia Lavin

Every socio-historical field produces a building type that singularly expresses the multiple forces that combine to produce the field itself. Whether it be the public bath of the late Roman empire, the Medieval cathedral, or the royal palace of the Age of Absolutism, each of these structures exemplifies the episteme that allowed it to gain prominence. The rise of modernity has made the identification of the building that holds this position of privilege an increasingly difficult task. The proliferation of building types, the development of new technologies, and the weakening of clearly definable cultural hegemonies have produced competition between art forms and other social artifacts, diminishing the capacity of any single phenomenon to assert its dominance. In view of Benjamin's observations that in a modern context architecture is perceived only through a state of distraction, it would seem that an effort to locate the building type best positioned to illuminate prevailing social and historical concerns would be futile since all buildings have been exiled to the peripheral vision of this new world.[1] At present no singularly expressive building type emerges clearly from this field of extreme conflict, but the work in Re: American Dream suggests that the dwelling may merit particular consideration precisely because it defines a site marked by the modern struggle for order.

Of the many forms of modern dwelling, the single-family house might be described as the type most irrelevant to the pressing concerns of contemporary architecture. Economically wasteful, politically suspect, and often formally bankrupt, the very idea seems nostalgic. At the same time, however, particularly in the United States and more particularly in southern California, the single-family house is the engine that drives a machine which is leaving tracks of tremendous consequence. The social dream of which the house is an essential component is not just visualized in the landscape of the imagination but is realized on almost every street of the American city. The number of such structures still being produced attests to the persistent quest for individualized and isolated interiority: the projects in Re: American Dream

1 Walter Benjamin, "The Work of Art in the Age of Mechanical Reproduction," in Illuminations (New York, 1968), 217-252.

address this need in ways that range from an emphasis on private courtyards tightly bound by perimeter walls to a general de-emphasis on the street as public space. The degree to which this building type is antithetical to conventional notions of urban form, however—an antithesis that has produced rampant suburbanization and social alienation—simultaneously reveals the deep complicity between the old single-family house and the new forces generating what is called the "postmodern condition."[2] In fact, what should logically be an antiquated building type has increasingly become the site of the most radical formal experimentation in architecture. It is precisely the collision of progressive and retrogressive vectors within the single-family house that lends it significance far greater than the parameters of the house itself.

The work in Re: American Dream reveals the increasingly complex form of importance in the social field that the single-family house has been acquiring since the eighteenth century, when certain fundamental aspects of modern sociality were invented. The key to this innovation was the substitution of convention for nature as the principle organizing human interaction. Society was no longer thought to embody effortlessly an order received from nature but was seen to construct its own order out of principles simply extrapolated from nature. As a result, differences previously held to be natural, such as those distinguishing aristocrat from commoner, were replaced by rationalized notions of social equality: two men each with the right to vote. The use of reason to denature nature itself, however, had paradoxical implications: the goal of rational order in the public sphere demanded that the private individual be valued but, at the same time, required that this private individuality not impinge on the pristine abstractness of a public realm populated by absolute equals.[3] These paradoxical developments had a clear architectural counterpart in the Abbé Laugier's exaltation of the primitive hut as a model for architecture.[4] He valued this structure of natural simplicity because it contained the raw stuff from which rational principles in harmony with social

2  On postmodernism in this context, see in particular Jean-François Lyotard, **The Postmodern Condition: A Report on Knowledge** (Minneapolis, 1984) and Frederic Jameson, "Postmodernism, or The Cultural Logic of Late Capitalism," in **New Left Review,** 146: 53-92, 1984.

3  On the conceptualization of the public sphere in the eighteenth century, see Jürgen Habermas, **The Structural Transformation of the Public Sphere: An Inquiry into a Category of Bourgeois Society,** trans. T. Burger in association with F. Lawrence (Cambridge, MA, 1989), and Roger Chartier, **The Cultural Origins of the French Revolution,** trans. L.G. Cochrane (Durham and London, 1991).

4  Marc-Antoine Laugier, **An Essay on Architecture,** trans. Wolfgang and Anni Hermann (Los Angeles, 1977; first published in 1753 as **Essai sur l'architecture**). See also Wolfgang Hermann, **Laugier and Eighteenth Century French Theory** (London, 1962).

convention could be constructed. While built out of natural materials and by men in a state of nature, the hut did not serve as an image of the power of nature to engender the architecture of society. Rather the hut offered proof of how the intervention of human reason could create order—social as well as architectural—where nature had made nothing but wilderness.

When Laugier called on architects never to forget the image of the primitive hut he had in mind the design of public buildings for the most part, but the primitive hut was above all a single-family house.[5] Indeed, Laugier shared with Rousseau the notion that the nuclear family was the basic building block out of which society was composed. The primitive hut therefore exemplified the moment when a device for ordering architecture became synonymous with a device designed to order society rather than reflect a natural social order. This synonymity, however, has resonated with conflict throughout the history of modern architecture. The conflation of social order with the order of an individual house assigned to architecture the task of negotiating the complex relation between the public and the private. From the moment the single-family house was invented, its design was burdened with the need to reinforce individual integrity while simultaneously demonstrating the individual's relation to a larger social continuum. This conflict is reenacted with the design of every dwelling. No house can escape the fact that its sanctity as a private interior in which the most intimate aspects of life are performed and where the personal politics of identity are defined will be compromised by the intrusion of public notions of order and reason. Even if physically and psychically removed from other human beings and their shelters, the interiority of a private retreat inevitably reaches a point where it confronts the public realm. This intrusive confrontation often takes the form of architecture and is often performed by the architect.

The nature of this confrontation in the modern world began to crystallize when the design of a house was multiplied, conceptually, to produce the design of housing. The modern city is the spatial

5 The fullest discussion of the many cultural roles played by the primitive hut is to be found in Joseph Rykwert's **On Adam's House in Paradise** (New York, 1972).

Order in the House

counterpart to this moment of crystallization, for the urban terrain is where the private order of the individual is most intensely juxtaposed with the social order of the public sphere. As urban populations escalated during the nineteenth century, this intensity burgeoned with two seemingly contradictory results. On the one hand, the "masses" were housed in tenements that, with some variations in their urban configuration, were characterized above all by their large number of utterly undifferentiated units. Individuals were housed and thus valued on some level, but differences between individuals and the inequities they revealed were decisively repressed. At the same time, the more mobile classes moved out of urban centers in an effort to preserve the sanctity of their homes. The stylistic expression of this effort, significantly contemporaneous to the uniform tenement, was historical eclecticism. This apparent celebration of difference and individuality through formal variety revealed only the underlying homogeneity of suburban exclusiveness and thus paralleled the repression of heterogeneity taking place in the city.

The inadequacy of nineteenth-century strategies encouraged the Modern Movement to further erase difference—difference between city and country, between classes, and between houses and housing. Le Corbusier's Villa Savoye of 1929 and housing project in Pessac of 1925, for example, are designed according to a fundamentally similar architectural order despite their profoundly distinct contextual, economic, and social conditions. The International Style imposed an even more aggressive formal unity in an effort to support social unity and pursued transparency in an effort to dissolve the barriers separating public and private space. Despite widespread criticism of the results, subsequent developments, particularly in the United States, have not met with greater success. Psychological and cultural attachments to the traditional single-family house, for example, led to the reinvention of historical prototypes but also to a consequent contextual and temporal dislocation.[6] Attempts to make large numbers of single-family houses

Re: American Dream

6 It is worth noting that many current celebrations of nineteenth-century eclecticism as the best model for insuring variety in residential developments is based on a rather profound misreading of the historical prototype. While eclecticism surely did lend formal variety to otherwise similar buildings, the variations were unified above all by their historicity. From a nineteenth-century point of view—a view deeply informed by the historical imagination—the continuity established by the historicity of eclecticism would have been much more apparent and important than differences between historical styles.

[ 1 2

cohere by multiplying them in housing tracts has resulted in the exopolis—endless seas of buildings in which the desire for individual expression has been perverted into a need to be indistinguishable.[7] For the most part, the complexities that converge in the American house have been reiterated and exacerbated rather than resolved by strategies that have indeed produced architectural and social order. Once established, however, this order is visibly problematic.

The work in Re: American Dream constitutes an important effort to confront the questions raised but not answered by the evolution of modern habitation. The selection of the single-family house as a focus of study does not continue the celebration of the building type as a removed laboratory for purely formal research but recognizes the house as the site where social and architectural concerns are most intimately connected. All the architects involved chose to address this issue through urban densification and by intensifying the privatization of the city's social space. Their choice therefore reflects how this building type remains situated precisely at the divide between the public and private realms, the site it has occupied since its invention in the eighteenth century. The exhibition construes the house as in an equivocal position and in need of compromise. For example, the American Dream is fundamentally about the independence of the house, but Re: American Dream counters with evidence that there is no such thing as an absolutely independent house—each dwelling in this exhibition is presented as an individual unit inexorably linked to others. At the same time, however, none of the exhibitors have developed master plans or urban schemes on a scale more ambitious than that of a single Los Angeles block. Each project attempts to mediate between the desire for land ownership and the urban consequences of conspicuous consumption. All acknowledge the automobile and none celebrate it. The history of the city is remembered, either because it is used as a site for archaeology, its general configurations are preserved, or its traditional building types recollected, but

7 On the concept of exopolis, see Edward W. Soja. "Inside Exopolis: Themes Screened in Orange County," in M. Sorkin. ed., Variations on a Theme Park: Scenes from the New American City ( New York. 1992 ).

Order in the House

the future of the city is not anticipated. These series of decisions that favor compromise suggest that architecture has become uncomfortable with the degree to which its potential to assist society by producing order depends on the degree to which it is willing to intrude by imposing order.

The most profound issue confronting contemporary architecture is the fact that the cultural importance of the discipline that enabled architecture to take meaningful action was historically derived from a faith in a building's capacity to produce order—in itself and for society. Today, however, the very concept of order has become suspect. The denaturalization of language, context, time, and the human associated with the postmodern condition is increasingly revealing the ideological basis of order in efforts not to equalize but to eradicate difference.[8] Order is rapidly retreating as a means of insuring personal liberty and emerging as a source of social repression and control. The wide variety of projects in this exhibition all demonstrate in different ways the impact on architecture being made by this new understanding of "order" as a social construct with only contingent value. Some projects attempt to mitigate images of order by legislating variety or with schemes that require the imposition of random elements before they can be considered complete. One design lays bare the militaristic potential of order through iconic representation while others suggest a celebration of the liberating potential of disorder. Together, however, the projects in the exhibition indicate that what has been decried as the diminished importance of architecture in the social field is neither reflected in nor caused by an inability to produce order. Rather, what is suggested is an unwillingness to impose architectural order and a willingness to explore the idea that social order is a desire that can no longer be ordered but only dreamt.

8 For a discussion of these aspects of postmodernism and their relation to the critique of order currently being developed in a variety of cultural fields, see N. Katherine Hayles. *Chaos Bound: Orderly Disorder in Contemporary Literature and Science* (Ithaca and London, 1990).

# Re-Visualizing the Dream:

John Kaliski

## Los Angeles and the Future of the Single-Family House

The houses and the automobiles are equal figments of a great dream, the dream of the urban homestead, the dream of a good life outside of the squalors of the European type of city, and thus a dream that runs back not only into the Victorian railway suburbs of earlier cities, but also to the country-house culture of the fathers of the US Constitution...Los Angeles cradles and embodies the most potent current version of the great bourgeois vision of the good life in a tamed countryside...[1]

There is the theoretical American dream of the one-family house, wearing a bit thin, and the applied one, that depends on continued ingenuity, resourcefulness, and neighborliness...Here is a test of our national character: to devise a process of improving and perfecting American housing that can satisfy many different constituencies, a process that can give the phrase "American dream" new meaning.[2]

Just as space, time, and matter delineate and encompass the essential qualities of the physical world, spatiality, temporality, and social being can be seen as the abstract dimensions which together comprise all facets of human existence. More concretely specified, each of these abstract existential dimensions comes to life as a social construct which shapes empirical reality and is simultaneously shaped by it.[3]

Los Angeles, as a city form, is increasingly difficult to classify. The broad generalizations used by pundits and commentators from other places never quite add up today. The self-assuredness which marked Reyner Banham's classifications in Los Angeles: The Architecture of Four Ecologies—"Surfurbia," "Foothills," "The Plains of Id," and "Autopia,"—while still valid, have taken on a sense of age, like wrinkled skin exposed to too much sun.[4] The Los Angeles "seen/scene" today is an image from a mirror cracked, not by being dropped or suddenly subjected to seismic shear, but by the inevitable fact of its glass liquidity thinning, thickening, and finally splintering, even as the reflection holds.[5]

Though Los Angeles's fabled topography of palm-tree-lined streets, single-family bungalows with backyard fruit trees, cruisers rumbling down straight-arrow fast-food-lined commercial strips,

2 Dolores Hayden. Redesigning the American Dream: The Future of Housing, Work, and Family Life (New York. 1986). 175.

3 Edward W. Soja. Postmodern Geographies: The Reassertion of Space in Critical Social Theory (London. 1990). 25.

5 Soja. 221. "The seen/scene is that of a new geography of modernization, an emerging postfordist urban landscape..." Soja's book, like much apocolyptic Los Angeles literature, prefigured a great conflagration, but few were prepared for the intensity and scope of the King Rebellion of April 1992.

4 See Banham.

1 Reyner Banham. Los Angeles: The Architecture of Four Ecologies (New York. 1978). 238.

and ever-present sunshine giving way to sunsets casting orange shadows on surrounding mountains is still visible, these potent images powerfully disguise extraordinary social and physical urban evolution. Of course, the statistics of change never tell the whole story, nor, absent as they are of human will, do they point the way towards the future. However, they do illustrate an onrush of quickening demographic and spatial transformation which too often overwhelms the ability of social, political, and economic institutions to devise coping strategies even as reactionary elements resist change by devising increasingly authoritarian restrictions on personal freedom.[6] Los Angeles finds itself engaged in a tempestuous debate about turf, its storied landscape a holy grail contested between those who would defend it at any cost and those who desire to transform it but have yet to grab control.

To question the mirage of this American dreamscape has always been a popular pursuit. One need only read the dark novels of Raymond Chandler,[7] be familiar with the paranoid African-American landscapes described in Chester Himes's If He Hollers Let Him Go,[8] or experience the cinematic nightmare of extrapolated social and technical disfunction in Ridley Scott's Blade Runner[9] to be reminded of this city's deeply mined noir tradition.[10] While every city has its seamy underbelly, for the past forty years Los Angeles's boosters were always able to slough off its nagging problems given prosperity, federally primed defense-oriented growth, and access to seemingly unlimited supplies of cheap labor, cheap mortgages, and cheap land. In the last five years, however, a rapid decline in the ready supply of land and money (if not cheap labor) has accelerated, producing voiced disquiet amongst increasing numbers of individuals and groups. For too many, 1992 marked the year when life in Los Angeles too closely imitated a noir tale. The hard facts of a decade's expansion and growth point to the dissolution of what up until the mid-1980's was still a commonly heard belief that this city was the physical embodiment of the American Dream.

6 Recently, the city of San Fernando, in cooperation with former LA County District Attorney Ira Reiner, passed a law prohibiting suspected gang members from the city's public parks. Jerry Silver, president of the Encino Homeowners Association, has proposed that newcomers to Los Angeles be required to show proof that they have lived in another big city such as Detroit, Cleveland, or Pittsburgh (see **Daily Commerce,** 7/8/91).

7 See especially Raymond Chandler's **The Little Sister.**

8 Chester Himes, **If He Hollers Let Him Go** (New York, 1986).

9 Blade Runner is based upon Phillip Dick's **Do Androids Dream of Electric Sheep.**

10 The best essay on LA noir is undoubtedly Chapter One, "Sunshine or Noir?" in Mike Davis, **City of Quartz: Excavating the Future in Los Angeles** (New York, 1990).

Re: American Dream

At first glance, Los Angeles remains true to its mythic ideal. Assuming a flat Cartesian grid, Los Angeles has 3.5 million people distributed across five hundred square miles and reaches a density of 7,000 persons per square mile, which for purposes of comparison is equivalent to the density, if not character, of Staten Island, New York's "rural" borough.[11] The bucolic myth of California's largest city is further reinforced when one spreads its 1,300,000 dwelling units across this idealized plain and realizes a residential density of just 4.4 dwelling units per acre.[12] This abstraction of statistics almost matches the actual built form of huge swaths of Los Angeles, "platted" in the early twentieth century with single-family house lots, fifty feet wide by one hundred fifty feet deep. The endurance, visibility, and popular acceptance of this building pattern throughout Los Angeles, in neighborhoods that span class, ethnic, and racial divisions, in part explains the persistence of the view by both those who live here and those who do not that Los Angeles remains a landscape of domestic opportunity which provides a home for every family within an urbanized Garden of Eden.

Los Angeles, of course, is not an idealized Cartesian plane. Indeed, the built form of this city less and less resembles the idyllic apparition that is suggested when residential densities are manipulatively spread across an abstracted geography, or based upon a myopia bounded by that wedge of land between La Brea Avenue to the east and Santa Monica Bay to the west, the Santa Monica Mountains to the north and the Santa Monica Freeway to the south. However, the degree to which Los Angeles in the last twenty years has become a dense, highly urbanized metropolis, albeit with a difference, is startling even to those who are astute observers of this place.

The rapid urbanization of Los Angeles is best illustrated by the 1990 Census which indicates that census tracts just to the west of the central business district are approaching population densities of 78,000 people per square mile, a fifty percent increase since 1980, and more or less equivalent to the average population

11  Steven Flusty kindly collected statistics on population density for New York and Los Angeles which are from the U.S. Department of Commerce. Bureau of the Census. 1988 County City Databook.

12  Los Angeles Times. August 25.1991.

Re-Visualizing the Dream

density of Manhattan.[13] Factoring in the city's overall population increase since 1980 of 17%, it is not surprising that older neighborhoods of single-family houses, duplexes, triplexes, and quads rapidly give way to denser multi-family housing. Throughout the city, the change in community character is traumatic as new construction, in conformance with Los Angeles's zoning code, increases dwelling densities from 10 to 20 to 40 to 80 dwelling units per acre.[14] The result, once again borrowing the New York analogy, is more akin to the densities if not the daily routines and architectural typologies of neighborhoods typified by block after block of three-, four-, and five-story walkups found in Queens, Brooklyn, and parts of Manhattan. While the greatest portion of Los Angeles's landscape, residential or otherwise, remains devoted to the free-standing single-family house with landscaped front, rear, and side yards, the vast majority of new housing and emerging inner-city communities are formed with higher density building types which physically, symbolically, and politically challenge those neighborhoods where Los Angeles's expected built environment remains.

Buildings and density quantified are merely the physical manifestation of the soulful human changes which charge the tenseness of Los Angeles's urban space. Anglos, the bedrock of Reyner Banham's "Middle West raised to the flashpoint,"[15] have diminished as a percentage of the population, if not yet influence, from over 60% to just 37% of the city's population, while a nascent "new majority" of Hispanics (40%), African Americans (13%), and Asians (9%) gradually assumes increasing political power and questions the prerogatives of business as usual.[16] Increasingly the main business questioned is the economic and racial dynamics of residential real estate. This is not surprising, for as Los Angeles's population grows and shifts in terms of ethnicity, fewer than one-fifth of the households are left able to afford or find the means to purchase a single-family house[17] while more than 40% spend more than one third of their incomes on rent.[18] Those who desire a new

13 LA Weekly, August 2-8, 1991. See also note 11.

14 This estimate is based upon the conversion of single-family house neighborhoods to multi-family house neighborhoods where the underlying Los Angeles City zoning is R3 or R4.

15 Banham, 25.

16 From "1990 Census - Preliminary Results," prepared by the City of Los Angeles Department of Planning.

17 Affordability data was compiled by Steven Flusty from the California Association of Realtor's affordability index for the Los Angeles metropolitan region.

18 Los Angeles Times, September 25, 1991.

"starter" home have little choice but to move to residential tracts located at the periphery of the metropolitan sprawl, forcing many to endure long commutes back to the job-rich core of the region.[19] Anecdotal horror stories abound of two-income households in rapidly developing desert communities who abandon children to daycare or school before dawn. Each income-earner then commutes two hours, only to repeat the numbing trip back home at the end of the day, and finally, after sunset, open the front door, too exhausted to do anything but microwave dinner and put the kids and then themselves to sleep, all for the priviledge of owning a piece of the dream. While this lifestyle may be acceptable to those that choose, and can afford, to endure it, 1990 Census data indicates that Anglos are far more likely to be in a position to buy one of these peripheral homes than Latinos and Blacks, further exacerbating the perceived and real differences between social groupings.

Compounding racial divisions is the disappearence of high-skill, blue-collar manufacturing jobs, resulting in a decrease in the number of male workers earning between $20,000 and $40,000 per year, even as thousands of low-skill or no-skill jobs are created at the bottom of the income range.[20] Many households thus find themselves only one or two paychecks away from being forced out of homes onto Los Angeles County's streets: streets which contain up to 250,000 homeless people, one third of them families. Meanwhile thousands of immigrants with few resources and limited skills are among those who continue to arrive in the city at the rate of 25,000 families per year, many of them forced to double- and triple-up in small apartments, garages, or old trailers hauled into bungalow backyards and displacing the formerly ubiquitous orange, grapefruit, and lemon trees.[21]

The rate of Los Angeles's population growth has simply outpaced the ability of developers and public agencies to keep up with the demand for housing. City officials estimate that the city is falling short by an estimated 15,000 dwelling units per year.[22] Yet, in a city where the population is exploding, land is scarce, and

19 The best descriptions of the Los Angeles region's imbalance of jobs in relation to housing is found in data compiled by the Southern California Association of Governments.

20 Los Angeles Times, July 28, 1991.

21 Los Angeles Times, August 25, 1991.

22 Los Angeles Times, July 28, 1991.

Re-Visualizing the Dream

decent affordable housing is difficult to find, planners and politicians are paralyzed by a stasis caused by those who insist upon the efficacy of the mythic built status quo, even as Los Angeles becomes increasingly dense and its excess residential zoning capacity dwindles to less than 100,000 units, a five-year supply.[23] Housing thus becomes both the text and sub-text of political rhetoric and emerges as a defining issue in the great debate about the future built form of Los Angeles, a debate which reveals both the substance and the ephemeral nature of our image of the American dream house, and our ability to implement it.

The traditional solution to growth—densification—is increasingly resisted by community groups because dense buildings are perceived to generate choking traffic and curbside parking problems, are considered physically inappropriate when juxtaposed against existing single-family- and even multi-family-house neighborhoods, and, though rarely articulated, because denser housing types symbolically stand for the rapid intrusion of people of different colors and languages who are perceived to represent a challenge to the hegemony of homeowner values. This latter paranoia is only fed when the newcomers are people of low income and the specter of dropping land values is raised in anguish-filled community halls. If on the one hand increased density (or as it is sometimes called in Los Angeles, "manhattanization")[24] is resisted, few, including most of the spokespeople for neighborhood associations, will admit to an agenda of no growth. Instead one hears talk of "managed growth," "green growth," "sustainable growth," and "jobs/housing balance," all two-dimensional strategies which accomodate expansion, as long as it is someplace else.

In fact, Los Angeles's planners never meant for the city to "manhattanize." Indeed, for the past twenty years the city of Los Angeles's official typology of growth has been a multi-nodal "centers" approach. The centers concept was meant to guide growth towards high density mixed-use cores and leave the vast majority of the city's land for sprawling suburban tracts of single-family

23 Los Angeles Times, August 25, 1991.

24 One anti-growth group has labeled themselves "Not Yet New York".

Re: American Dream

homes. At least, on paper, the centers concept is a brilliant compromise which preserves the spatial hegemony of Anglo homeowners while simultaneously maintaining their ability to individually participate as prospective developers in the speculative development of high-density centers where they never have to live. In actual practice, neither politicians, developers, nor the planning beaurocracy was able to implement, much less enforce, this vision. Mass transit, intended to connect the new centers, was not implemented quickly enough. Centers did occur, but not where the planners expected. Rather they occurred where the cars could go. Finally, there was little incentive for Los Angeles's governing officials, dependent on developer contributions, to synchronize the centers-oriented General Plan, which required the lowering of densities, with an older, post-World War II blanket of existing and excessive density allowances.

Los Angeles today is traffic congestion, sterile office parks, and shopping malls with acres of parking, pockmarked by "centers" that have few residents. Everywhere one consistently encounters the rapid transformation of low-scale neighborhoods as property owners and developers cash in their entitlements. In short, the end product of twenty years of growth is a crisis symbolized by the failure of urban form. To put it bluntly, Los Angeles, celebrated for its natural beauty and ideal climate, is becoming ugly, and while pockets of extraordinary vitality and charm suggest the promise of decades past, the collective daily life of most of its citizenry takes place in an environment which is increasingly hostile to life's patterns and daily needs.

Neither European precedents nor the new towns of the neo-traditional planners can provide models for the needed evolution of Los Angeles's urban form. The concentrations of power and capital required for the success of these prototypes can only be brought to bear on virgin landscapes.[25] Today, those designing Los Angeles have little choice but to accept its existing context and reformulate the idea of its basic urban building blocks. To address the crisis of

25  In urbanized Los Angeles the confirming example of the need for tabula rasa landscapes when designing "new towns" is the proposed new town, Playa Vista. The project consists of eight hundred acres on an exisiting wetland and abandoned airfield, designed by neo-traditionalists Andres Duany and Elizabeth Plater-Zyberk. with Moule Polyzoides and Associates, for developers Maguire Thomas Partners.

Re-Visualizing the Dream

this city means fundamentally to reinvent the form, if not the ideal, of its most important constituent part, the single-family house. The mutation in space of the single-family house over time provides the best means to incrementally re-form Los Angeles, parcel by parcel, in a way that acknowledges the gravity of the current housing crisis yet is accepting of its physical traditions. In essence, the American Dream must be redefined to fit today's diversely composed households within the context of a vast urban metropolis.

In Los Angeles, the reinvention of the dream will necessarily have to provide more urban housing for more people in less space while maintaining a sense of privacy and the presence of the individual homestead set within a garden. Toward this end, practical solutions have been proposed which maintain the character of a spread-out city composed of tightly knit neighborhoods. Among these are the loosening of codes to encourage the construction of backyard or over-garage "granny flats." This simple change in the zoning code would create a means to begin enforcing minimum health and building code standards in the currently illegal garage apartments of an estimated 50,000 Angelenos. At the same time it would provide an incentive to small households to improve their properties for the supplemental income potential. More aggressive manipulations of the code could selectively allow for the building of small rental units within the footprint of existing single-family houses. This would allow individuals the security of additional income and perhaps companionship as they grow older and life's needs change. Predictably these concepts, which preserve the physical character of single-family-house neighborhoods yet allow for the efficient yield of additional dwelling units, have thus far run into the values of homeowner groups fearful of changes perceived to threaten the value of property.[26]

More experimental approaches which maintain the character of low-scale neighborhoods by increasing residential densities only at the neighborhood's periphery have just begun to be explored. Los Angeles's great gridded network of under-utilized commercial

26. Homeowners forced the removal of accessory unit language from Los Angeles's recently adopted "Comprehensive Housing Affordability Strategy." This document, produced by the city's Department of Housing Preservation and Production, is probably the best current source for information regarding Los Angeles's housing crisis.

27 See Douglas R. Suisman. Los Angeles Boulevard: Eight X-Rays of the Body Public. (Los Angeles. 1989).

strips creates natural community boundaries and edges along which higher-density, mixed-use projects could be built.[27] Mid-rise housing and offices over shops within easy walking distance of adjacent low-scale neighborhoods could provide the basis of a new Los An-geles urban typology. Neither a center nor a suburb, "boulevard" Los Angeles could be a great grid of urban life and amenities lacing and overlooking a finer network of quiet, older, lower-scale residential neighborhoods with tree-lined streets. This future Los Angeles could be implemented through an inclusionary zoning, which downzones existing neighborhoods but increases residential bonus densities along major boulevards and transportation corridors in exchange for the provision of affordable housing units.

While selective rezonings could allow for increased mixed-use development along boulevard corridors and preserve interstitial single-family residential communities, those places where urban lifestyles and densities already exist will have to evolve if Los Angeles's goals for increasing the amount of affordable housing are to be met. This task presents perhaps the greatest challenge, for Los Angeles's densest communities, such as Hollywood, Koreatown, and Westlake, are reservoirs of low-income housing and are, therefore, vulnerable to demolition and new construction, or rehabilitation and conversion to market-rate units, as land values rise. In these parts of the city the confluence of a lack of public housing policy, restrictive building codes, high construction costs, and high densities conspire to form the repetitious construction on street after street of mindless four-story boxes. These are perched over two stories of open parking deck, with little open space save for five-foot side yards and fifteen-foot front yards. Low-income households are displaced as buildings with almost no family units are built. Streets become garage alleys. Children are left with no place to play. Basic assumptions of twentieth-century housing such as natural light and ventilation become precious luxuries. These conditions demand the invention of new building prototypes which, repeated through space, create a reformed physical urban landscape.

Unfortunately, most schemes which organically reinvent the form of Los Angeles are simply two-dimensional planning concepts. Homeowners, housing advocates, planners, and even architects debate broad issues of city form without ever showing each other that which they are describing. Politicians find themselves brokering development compromises on a case-by-case basis through an exquisite choreography of special interest groups that leaves few satisfied and never truly addresses the larger issues. Thus, Los Angeles is gradually defined through a myopic incremental decision-making process that results, at best, in a few individual projects of merit in a demeaned, devalued, and polluted landscape of physical and psychic despair. Given these conditions, the public, which still vividly observes the remains of a city in a "tamed countryside,"[28] naturally remains suspicious of those who promise that a better urban future will be realized through growth. America's second largest city now desperately needs new physical models of growth, in essence a new "image of the city,"[29] in turn engendering a new consensus, breaking the deadlock between those whose vision of Los Angeles is two decades old and those who blindly seek a vision but do not have the form-giving skills to invent one.

If the single-family house remains a potent image of the American Dream, and Los Angeles a city shaped by the consequences of its form, then this city today is an ideal place to test new forms of the dream. The challenge for architects is not only to participate in the dreaming but to contribute a believable physical model of a Los Angeles where homes and neighborhoods stretch below the mountains to the ocean, are shaped by an understanding of climate and topography, and are bounded by the reality of an urban Los Angeles with urban boulevards, urban places, and urban amenities and pleasures. What architects must call for, work towards, and visualize is the reinvention in multiple forms of this city's fundamental physical and social cell, the single-family house, such that its repetitions will shelter all individuals within an urban vitality which retains the promise of a city set within a garden.

28 Banham, 238.

29 Kevin Lynch, The Image of the City (Cambridge, 1960).

structure or enlargement.

**ont Yard** — There shall be a front yard of n
' the depth of the lot, but such front yard need no
however, that where all of the developed lots w
vary in depth by not more than 10 feet compri
ne frontage, the minimum front yard depth shall
he front yards of such lots. Where there are two
ons of developed lots comprising 40 percent
each of which has front yards that vary in depth h
ne minimum front yard depth shall be the avera
s of that combination which has the shallowest a
ng the required front yard, buildings located on h
ar half of lots, or on lots in the "C" or "M" Zor
provided, however, that nothing contained in this
d to require front yards which exceed 40 feet in c
*Jo. 139,155, Eff. 10/16/69.)*

ey lots the minimum front yard may be the averag
l for the adjoining interior lot and the required sic
e of a reversed corner lot, but such minimum fron
ance of not more than 65 feet from the rear lot lin
t, beyond which point the front yard specifie
h shall apply. Where existing buildings on either
lots are located nearer to the front or side lot line
by this Article, the yards established by such e
used in computing the required front yard for a

**ide Yards** — For a main building not more tha
ere shall be a side yard on each side of said bu
feet, except that where the lot is less than 50 f
may be reduced to 10 percent of the width of t
less than three feet in width. For a building more
, one foot shall be added to the width of such si
l story above the second story. *(Amended by Ord*

# Joint Statement

**The freestanding single-family dwelling** is the physical embodiment of the American Dream and has provided the ideal for the home in Los Angeles since the beginning of this century. Since World War II the city has welcomed a steady rate of growth without having to reconsider this ideal by expanding its boundaries and developing its freeway system. After fifty years the freeway and utility infrastructures continue to expand and housing development, pushed to the rim of the basin, threatens to overrun the desert. By the end of the second millenium Los Angeles will have reached its geographic limits.

**The population density** in a typical district of Los Angeles is one-tenth of that of a comparable district in Paris and one-thirtieth of that in Manhattan, and still we perceive that Los Angeles is "over-crowded." The experience of the last fifty years has shown that continual appropriation of virgin lands motivated by the desire to "escape" this condition is environmentally destructive and fails to address the real possibility that systemic problems underlie this perception. Clearly, the suburban structure upon which the city is founded must evolve.

**In the meantime** increasing density has intensified the physical and social complexities of the city. The population has become culturally diverse while the variety of family types has multiplied: research shows that single persons make up 24% of the households in Los Angeles and traditional nuclear families only 12%. Some areas of the city have become more desirable and therefore "pressurized" while others have been abandoned and left in a state of ruin. Commuting time has tripled since 1956, gridlock has become a household word, and parking an almost daily frustration.

**We believe** that in the face of the mounting housing crisis of metropolitan Los Angeles the proliferation of the simple tract house cannot continue. Furthermore, those building types which have emerged in response to demands for greater density such as the "ding-bat" apartment house and other crude build-to-the-limit by-products of zoning legislation have proven inadequate as alternatives to the ubiquitous detached house. These buildings increase the number of residents in certain areas, aggravating the perception of being over-crowded, and yet do little to contribute positively to life in the city.

We propose the Urban House as a meaningful alternative to the wasteful tract house and the oppressive apartment complex. Even if limited to the single lot the Urban House must consider the consequences of its multiplication within a vast and culturally diverse urban Los Angeles. It cannot be treated as a singular event in a conflict-free garden setting as was the case in the postwar era when the tract house was the ideal. We need to ask how the Urban House will relate to existing buildings, to the street system, infrastructures and superstructures already in place, and surrounding public and commercial realms of the city.

Still, the problem of the Urban House is not to be framed as merely a program for urban design in the "planning" sense of the word. It is first and foremost an issue of building design with economic, psychological, and symbolic implications. We frame the problem by asking how close we should live, how high, how we dine, bathe, sleep; what are the kinds of rooms we need and want, how do we reach them, where is the front door. The Urban House must consider the values we associate with the front lawn, the entertainment center, the things we accumulate in our homes. We ask how the Urban House will relate to other urban houses, to the ground, and to the sky.

The tract house admits light to its rooms through small windows and doors at its perimeter. In a climate where sunlight is abundant we ask how might the Urban House exploit the broader range of possibilities such as diaphanous or semi-transparent surfaces, baffles, transparent walls, and open-air apertures. The tract house has sloped tile or asphalt shingle roofs but in an arid climate we ask how might the Urban House use its roofs for elevated gardens or terraces. These are matters central to the questions of density, the economics of building, and the quality of life in the city—questions urban planning cannot ignore.

Finally, the Urban House must address the politics, pragmatics, and symbolic importance of individual property ownership so central to the American Dream. In the context of metropolitan Los Angeles we might conclude that Thomas Jefferson's agrarian ideal has irreconcilably collided with Adam Smith's capitalism. We choose instead to see this condition as rich in opportunity for peoples of all walks of life to live together in ways not originally envisioned in the formative years of the city. The Urban House must provide alternatives—in order that the city continue to prosper and its inhabitants live pleasurably and with dignity.

# Janek Bielski

Team: Carl Welty, Ate Atema, Kari Richardson, Mark Bielski, Carolee Toon, Wojtek Szaszor, Margaret Szalay, Charles Lee, Andy Bristol, Paul Neuhaus, Eli Bonerz, Martin Lewis, Toni Hopman

Innovative housing types are needed to bridge the gap between the ubiquitous land-inefficent single-family dwelling, which desperately relies on the automobile for its survival, and the replete yet ill-conceived "dingbat" apartment building, which has created dismal living conditions with minimal private open space. These two most common housing types in Los Angeles have proven to be a contributing factor in the deterioration of the quality of life in the city and outlying areas.

However, there are ways to build higher density housing without losing the qualities of the individual home or an intimate relation with generous open space—be it a private garden or communal courtyard. It is possible to build housing that allows for economic disparity on the same block, incorporating, for example, the needs of renters with those of property owners hoping to maximize the investment in their properties. By recognizing the peculiarities of a particular place, and responding to the need for diverse rental and ownership options, housing can be designed to address specific issues which may lead to a city of exceptionally diverse communities.

Perhaps one of the more contested issues in housing projects regards the role and relationship between the public and private realms within residential areas. The author accepts that the increasing privatization of residential areas is a reality within which we must operate. Therefore, the proposal maximizes the useable space of private properties, with the provision that interaction between neighbors can occur on more levels than simply the "public" or the "private."

The project is conceived in a way that allows residents to create shared spaces and facilities, as well as develop alternative housing types. The residents' relationships and priorities on the block are reflected in its open spaces, housing types, and amenities. At one extreme, the residents may choose to maximize the area of private property; on the other hand, through a series of property transactions, they may choose to develop communal functions incorporating recreational areas, day-care centers, workshops, or shared parking structures.

The project is a zoning proposal conceived spatially and incorporating diverse social conditions. The models and drawings are examples of the new zoning ordinance. The permutations within the proposed ordinance are inexhaustible. The site is flat, with no particular adjacent natural or cultural amenities. Therefore it is an introverted scheme, deferring to the sky and ground. The economic and demographic reality is diverse, and the proposal encourages that diversity. Finally, it responds to the climate of the region, being exceptionally conducive to outdoor life.*

The proposed zoning ordinance suggests a hybrid housing type—merging the detached single-family dwelling and the residential courtyard type. The hybrid type preserves the privileges and responsibilities of detached home-ownership while introducing a higher density (two to three times R1) with excellent land-use efficiency.

By splitting the typical 50' x 150' lot along its length, the wasteful side yard is eliminated, becoming a continuous twenty-eight-foot-wide garden or court along the length of the building (existing side yard property lines shift to the setback line of the adjoining property). By pushing the allowable building area to the existing front and rear property lines, the buildable area and the private garden space is increased,

thereby eliminating the wasteful front, side, and rear setback conditions.

The alternating solid-void
bars create an equivalence
between the building and the
landscape. The recurring garden
gives reprieve to the building,
providing an animated solid-void (building-garden) experience on the sidewalk. The outdoor space brings
plentiful sunlight and ventilation to every unit, as well as providing generous recreational spaces or medi-
tative places of repose. The quasi-courtyard is enclosed on two sides by building and on the other two
sides by hedges, fences, or walls, separating the units into private domains.

The block is transformed incrementally. Every attempt has been made to encourage individual
expression to satisfy a broad range of lifestyles, economic diversities, and aesthetic preferences.
Individual property owners have the option either to leave their houses "as is," or to implement changes
consistent with the proposed zoning code. The house may expand, rental units may be attached, or connec-
tions developed with one's neighbor—a strategy which mutates the parallel bars into "bridge buildings,"
courtyards, etc. Thus, another scale of making larger "places" within the block is possible by making
changes to one's house or creating conditions with one's neighbor(s).

The continual possibility of transformation is integral to the conception of the project. A more
sophisticated, perhaps computer-based, code would have to be implemented, possibly based on a point or
quota system—allowing only so many crossover units, third stories, etc. Bearing in mind that the role of
cars may change—perhaps a metro station will be built nearby—parking is considered in a more flexible
way: private garages, communal garages, and tandem parking are provided for some units, while no parking
is required of others.

The proposal is envisioned as one of many new housing proposals attempting to satisfy the various
existing and emerging demographic, economic, and landscape conditions of Los Angeles. The proposed new
zoning code was conceived in response to the indiscriminate building development which has had devastat-
ing effects on the quality of life and the environment in southern California. Addressing these issues, the
project suggests planning directives which create more options and opportunities for residents in Los
Angeles at the end of the twentieth century.

*In order to determine the building and landscape variations in the proposal, the presentation was based on a methodology which freed the design process
from the burden of continual formal "invention." Through a series of overlays from a map of southern California, particular information was extracted and
converted, to establish both building and landscape types, densities, and locations. This design methodology was developed only to demonstrate the variations possible in the proposed zoning concept. The resulting presentation is not intended as the final solution, but rather presents the inherent possibilities
of a zoning concept.

Single Lot

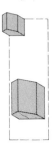  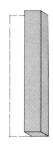

| Existing Building Configuration on a Typical Residential Lot on a Typical Block in Los Angeles | Proposed Building Configuration on Same Lot Within the Existing Zoning Code | Proposed Building Configuration on Same Lot Within the Proposed Zoning Code |
|---|---|---|
| House   1.250 Sq. Ft.   16.6% | House   2.420 Sq. Ft.   32.3% | House   2.900 Sq. Ft.   38.7% |
| Garage   400 Sq. Ft.   5.3% | Garage   400 Sq. Ft.   5.3% | Garage   400 Sq. Ft.   5.3% |
| Driveway   1.500 Sq. Ft.   20.0% | Driveway   500 Sq. Ft.   6.6% | Driveway   0 Sq. Ft.   0.0% |
| Side Yard   175 Sq. Ft.   2.4% (@ House) | Side Yard   550 Sq. Ft.   7.3% (@ House) | Side Yard   0 Sq. Ft.   0.0% |
| Front Yard   1.000 Sq. Ft.   13.4% | Front Yard   0 Sq. Ft.   0.0% | Front Yard   0 Sq. Ft.   0.0% |
| Private Yard   3.175 Sq. Ft.   42.3% (Back) | Private Yard   3.630 Sq. Ft.   48.5% (Back) | Private Yard   4.200 Sq. Ft.   56.0% |
| **Total Lot   7.500 Sq. Ft.** | **Total Lot   7.500 Sq. Ft.** | **Total Lot   7.500 Sq. Ft.** |

Properties

 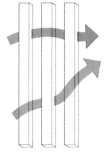 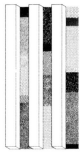 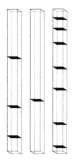 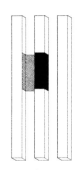

| North-South Orientation | Units Cross-Ventilated | Gardens Between Units | Simple Unit Division | Unit & Garden |
|---|---|---|---|---|

Types

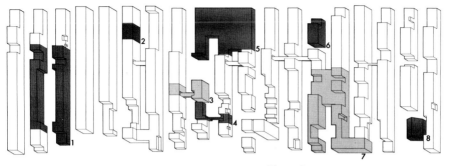

1 Courtyard
2 Bar Unit
3 Hybrid: Bar Unit/Detached Unit
4 Cross-Bar
5 Parking Structure
6 Detached
7 Hybrid: Courtyard/Workshop
8 Existing

Janek Bielski

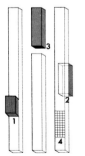

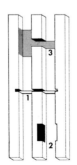
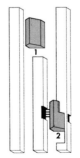
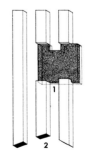

**Unit Permutations**
1 Above
2 Below
3 Detached
4 Terrace

**Parking**
1 Private
2 Tandem
3 Multiple

**Links**
1 Bridges
2 Niches
3 Breaks

**Existing Housing**
1 Isolated
2 Engaged

**Communal Space**
1 Recreational
2 Street-related

Incremental Densification of Block

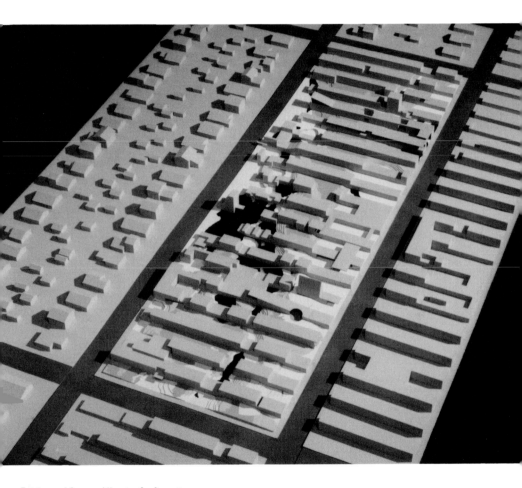

Existing and Proposed Housing Configurations

Ground Floor Plan

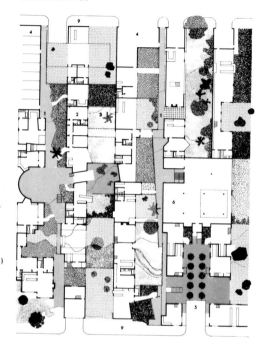

⊕  0 10  5'      50 ft.
   ⊢⊣⊔⊔       ⊣

1 Shared Access
2 Residence ( typical )
3 Garden / Courtyard ( typical )
4 On Grade Parking
5 To Subterranean Parking
6 Shared Workshop
7 Shared Lounge / Jacuzzi
8 Shared Recreational
9 Sidewalk

Section A

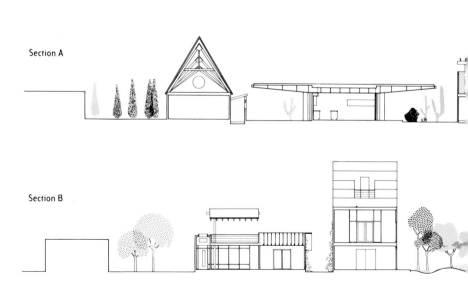

Section B

Second Floor Plan

Third Floor Plan

Janek Bielski

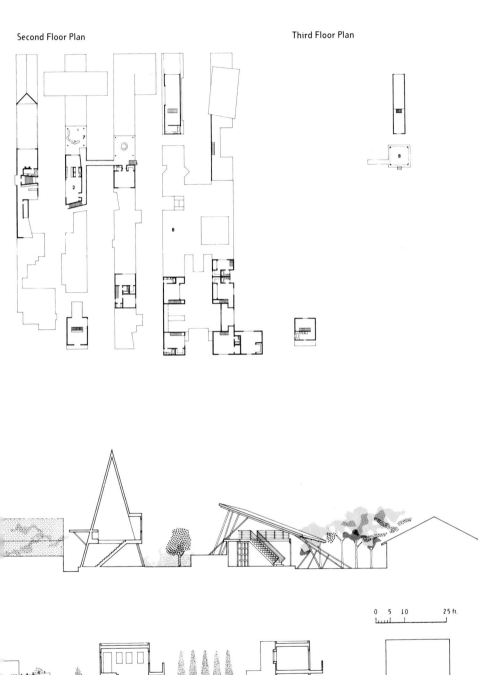

0  5  10      25 ft.

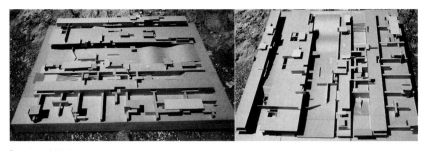

Segment of Block: Preliminary Model

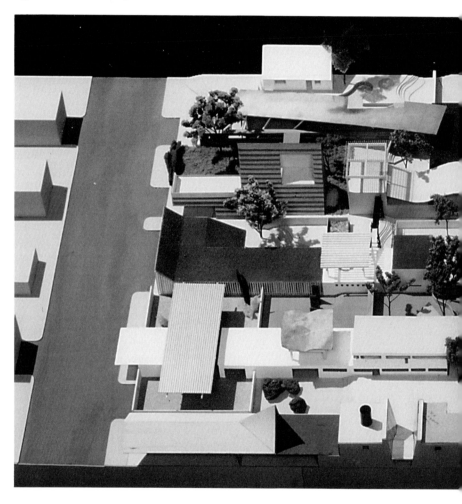

Segment of Block: Developed Model

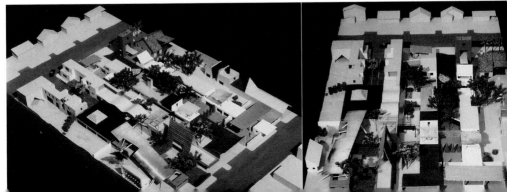

Janek Bielski

Discrete Scenarios

Janek Bielski

# COA: Central Office of Architecture

Team: Ron Golan, Eric A. Kahn, Russell N. Thomsen, (Principals.) David LeClerc

Re: American Dream

## An Incomplete Project: Towards A Recontextualization of Modernity and the Urban House Prototype in Los Angeles

Los Angeles, it should be understood, is not a mere city. On the contrary, it is, and has been since 1888, a commodity; something to be advertised and sold to the people of the United States like automobiles, cigarettes and mouth wash.[1]

—Morrow Mayo, Los Angeles (New York, 1933)

Densify or die

Los Angeles has seen unprecedented and rampant exploitation by hegemonous political and economic forces which dissolve the public realm of the city into a seamless horizontal experience of bankrupt formal gestures devoid of value either urbanistically or architecturally. Greed, in the form of the capitalist machine, combined with the concept of rampant frontierism,[2] have left Los Angeles in the hands of extraordinary rapists who control and continuously exploit the city toward solely speculative (financial, political) ends. This violence has left in its wake slums and decaying neighborhoods, victims of the continuous interruption and erasure of hierarchy as the measure of a legible and sentient experience within the grid of Los Angeles. Nostalgia for the specific myth of its own fictitious past creates a pervasive and amplified dementia which vividly portrays the misery and blasé attitude[3] of the contemporary urban experience. Los Angeles, lacking an awareness of its own essence,[4] lies directionless, forever folding in on itself, resulting in a pervasive homogeneity.

Morphologically, Los Angeles is a complex hybrid; its unstable and shifting form exists in a flux somewhere between the traditional European city model of fabric and corridor streets, and the modernist conception of the city as object-buildings in the park. The traditional city is primarily an experience of spaces defined by continuous walls of building, arranged in a way that emphasizes the figure of the void and de-emphasizes the building volumes. The modernist conception, espoused by Le Corbusier, is phenomenally an opposite model: it is one of discrete three-dimensional objects floating in space, amplifying their autonomy and individuality while defying gravity. Los Angeles, existing in that zone which simultaneously suggests and denies either or both of these models, posits perhaps a third alternative, that of the post-city. The condition of the post-city is characterized by the coexistence of contradictory and incompatible elements, causing an irresolvable aporia. The post-city, unable to make and differentiate constructed relationships, renders thin experience through an infinitely expanding and accelerating web of non-hierarchical traced paths. The previous definitions of city are superceded; the possibility of a totalizing portrait is eliminated, rendered inconceivable and inappropriate.

Primary Ordering Diagram

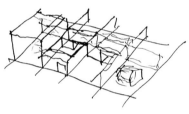

Preliminary Morphological Diagrams

It is impossible to say precisely when one can begin to speak of the existence of two distinct and bitterly conflicting modernities. What is certain is that at some point during the first half of the nineteenth century an irreversible split occurred between modernity as a stage in the history of Western civilization—a product of scientific and technological progress, of the industrial revolution, of the sweeping economic and social changes brought about by capitalism—and modernity as an aesthetic concept.[5]
—Matei Calinescu, Five Faces of Modernity

Calinescu describes a conception of modernity polarized by the irreconcilable opposition between two sets of values corresponding to "1) the objectified, socially measurable time of capitalist civilization (time as a more or less precious commodity, bought and sold on the market), and, 2) the personal, subjective, imaginative durée, the private time created by the unfolding of the 'self.' The

*Central Office of Architecture*

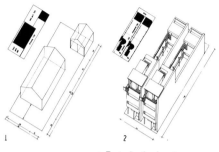

1 Typical suburban house:
1600 square feet on a 45' X
120' lot. Front and side yards,
along with required
setbacks result in 1125
square feet of private outdoor
space.

2 The urban prototype allows
for two units of 1600 square
feet each to occupy the same
lot size, while maintaining the
same amount of private outdoor space for each.

The units become mutually
dependent

latter identity of time and self constitutes the foundation of modernist culture."[6] The current pluralist condition of the postmodern has left Los Angeles in the unstable state of an urban palimpsest, a metropolitan text undergoing erasure and layering in such a way as to become the equivalent of a multiple-exposure photograph: ambiguous and open for multiple-readings at best, entropic noise at worst. A post-existentialist value system confuses the loss of the first principle, the reliable and definitive reference point (and for better or worse, a source of the collective will) with that of a solipsistic narcissism, symptomatic of a pathology brought on by the forces of late capitalism. The result is a vacuous condition that resists coherence and falsely relieves the citizen of responsibility to any larger, collective conception of the metropolis. Radical privatization, the ideology of consumption, fear of boredom, and the need for escape leaves contemporary metropolitan Los Angeles with a misconception of pluralism and chaos as freedom.[7]

Conditions within the instability of the modern urban condition are juxtaposed and played for their theatricality in Jacques Tati's film, Mon Oncle (1956). Monsieur Hulot lives in a penthouse above a typically quaint French place, where he has daily encounters with his neighbors. Hulot enjoys rotating his bedroom window in order to reflect sunlight into a neighbor's window, blinding a noisy pet parrot. His relationship to the city is one of exteriorization and interaction, situating Monsieur Hulot within both a morphologically and demographically stable part of the city. At the same time, in another part of the city, Hulot's well-off sister lives within a walled modernist compound where life becomes one of separation and repose from the experience of the city. The everyday experience is radically internalized resulting in an amplified response to its contained site. It is our assumption that one cannot play both sides in this scenario; housing in the city cannot simultaneously contain both of these conditions without contradiction. Radical privatization[8] on both the corporate and individual level has all but ended the need and desire for public space in metropolitan Los Angeles. Actual space in the unstable capitalist metropolis,[9] displaced by technological advancement and consequent alterations in socio-cultural phenomena, has been replaced with collapsed space.[10] The circumspect form of simulated space and communication networks exemplify the rapidity of transformation, organization, and simultaneity of communications, as well as the city's accelerated tempo of use, eclecticism, and the fetishism of technology.[11] These side effects of modernity, if not problematized, reduce the artistic experience of architecture to a pure object (an obvious metaphor for object-merchandise), where the criterion of economic obsolescence overrides all others.

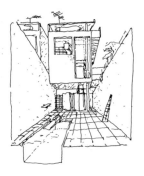

Alley Unit from courtyard

## Densify or Die

Faced with the reality that orgies of construction during economically ripe times have made a mess of our urban life, it seems imperative to stop and reflect through the critical act of the project itself, opening a window of optimism amidst the neglect and disinvestment that has plagued entire urban sectors. The critical architectural response must be one of opposition to Los Angeles's indiscriminate growth. While accepting the inherent contradictions of time and place, it must respond to them in a manner which adds hierarchy and, hence, legibility to the experience of the city.

Ridgeley Unit from courtyard

This work stands as a substantive contribution toward the establishment of a praxis regarding architectural interventions[12] within the grid of Los Angeles. It does not argue for the final form of the city, but instead postulates given a critical reading of the situation based on certain criteria. Judgments can then be made and directed toward a meaningful architectural intervention. The work is a hypothesis about the ordering of events, countering hegemonic political, social, and economic tendencies, and proposes with fixed and measured results a tenable model of future proposals for housing fabric within the city. Under such circumstances, what is needed is not the naive and nostalgic simulation of "the front porch" but instead "housing" as a proposition which reveals its own true presence based on values that critique the existing paradigm of both the structure of the individual dwelling and the morphology of the city. The formal and conceptual continuity of the intervention transcends

Central Office of Architecture

All this was designed in my husband's factory

its functionalist origin and becomes part of the memory of the city itself as it is traversed by both time and experience. The totalization of the block reinforces its ability to resist the shifting of the hegemonous forces which surround it. As an unexecuted project, the proposal seeks to free itself from specific zoning restrictions, the residue of archaic codes, in order to show that, with sober thinking and analysis, the problem of housing can be resolved in architectural form. Its representative form is meant to embody a coherent expression of our beliefs regarding the status of the role of architects working within a critical framework.

The unfolding evolution of the city cell or dwelling can be seen as the history of evolving a model for habitation. Le Corbusier's proclamation, "The house is a machine for living in"[13] demanded a paradigm shift away from what was clearly in his mind an outdated and wholly inhumane condition of life for modern humankind. It is a misreading to understand Corbusier's proclamation as one of supporting the machine aesthetic. It was clearly a demand for culture to come to grips with the logic and perfection of "a problem clearly stated" and the necessity of architecture and lifestyle to reconcile themselves with technology. The white villas then must be critiqued in relation to the active adaptation of the individual to technological reality and the new spatial conditions that such a reality imposes. Our intention is to reinvest space in the condition of modernity, space which has been occluded by the polarity described by Matei Calinescu. In order to escape the commodification of the "house" as a fetishistic autonomous object, as exemplified by the Case Study House program in Los Angeles in the late 1950s, we choose to focus on the morphology of the block and the house type as integral parts of the fabric of the city.[14] We believe in the tangible and clear achievement of the modernist project recontextualized, which leads to the conviction that it is far from bankrupt in its various contemporary manifestations, and that through our own comment we have progressed far from its Eurocentric origin.

The idea of "context" is seen conceptually as an equation where the value of the existing structure of

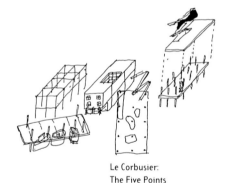

Le Corbusier:
The Five Points

the block is weighed against the value of the proposed intervention. The intervention exists as a critical discourse on urban housing and its relation to the city; it embraces the grid[15] as a basic organizational language in order to manifest a legible diagram that counters the intolerable situation which surrounds it.

The need to densify housing will bring about certain changes. Open space in residential quarters must be devoted either to streets or to real human activity instead of useless side and front yards. In order to achieve more density, buildings must have smaller footprints and consequently push upwards.

The increase in density will require a shift from the current definition of suburban space by trees, shrubs, and low fences to an urban definition of space by buildings, courts, and high walls. While increases in density will result in decreased use of the car, the car and house will remain inextricably linked.

The form of the American Dream embodied in the single-family detached suburban house is irreconcilable with the inevitable increase in population density and the potential for a quality urban experience. A new type of urban house must develop which retains the most important aspects of the American Dream: individual home and land ownership and the preservation of private space.

Ridgeley Unit from balcony

Ridgeley Unit interior from entry

Central Office of Architecture

## Notes

1 Quoted in Mike Davis. **City of Quartz: Excavating the Future in Los Angeles** (New York. 1990). 319.

2 Central Office of Architecture. "Los Angeles and the Curse of Bigness." in **Offramp** (Los Angeles. 1989).

3 "The essence of the blasé attitude (towards the city) consists of the blunting of discrimination. This does not mean that the objects are not perceived. as in the case with the half-wit. but rather. that the meaning and differing values of things. and thereby the things themselves. are experienced as insubstantial. They appear to the blasé person in an evenly flat and grey tone: no one object deserves preference over any other. This mood is the faithful subjective reflection of a completely internalized money economy...all things float with equal specific gravity in the constantly moving stream of money. All things lie on the same level and differ from one another only in the size of the area which they cover." Georg Simmel. "Die Grossstadt und das Geistesleben" (Dresden 1903). Eng. trans.. "The Metropolis And Mental Life" in **The Sociology of Georg Simmel**, trans. and ed. Kurt H. Wolff (New York. 1950). 409-424.

4 See Heidegger's lecture. "The Question Concerning Technology." His definition of "essence" shows that it does not simply mean what something is. but that it means further the way in which something pursues its course. the way in which it remains through time as what it is. It also must be understood as "presencing" or "coming to presence" which gives the word a contextual ref-

modern, all communicati

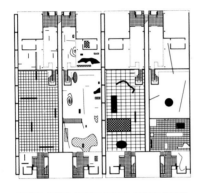

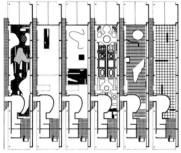

The courtyard becomes the potential site for the projection of the individual's need and desire for the manifestation of myth and ritual.

erence to time and becoming. Heidegger states: "Modern technology too is a means to an end. That is why the instrumental conception of technology conditions every attempt to bring man into the right relation to technology. Everything depends on our manipulating technology in the proper manner as a means. We will master it. The will to mastery becomes all the more urgent the more technology threatens to slip from human control."

5 Matei Calinescu, **Five Faces Of Modernity** (Durham, 1987), 41-42. He adds: "With regard to the first, bourgeois idea of modernity, we may say that it has by and large continued the outstanding traditions of earlier periods in the history of the modern idea. The doctrine of progress, confidence in the beneficial possibilities of science and technology, the concern with time (a measurable time, a time that can be bought and sold and therefore has, like any other commodity, a calculable equivalent to money), the cult of reason, and the ideal of freedom defined within the framework of an abstract humanism, but also the orientation toward pragmatism and the cult of action and success—all have been associated in various degrees with the battle for the modern and were kept alive and promoted as key values in the triumphant civilization established by the middle class. By contrast, the other modernity, the one that was to bring into being the avant-gardes, was from its romantic beginnings inclined toward radical antibourgeois attitudes. It was disgusted with the middle-class scale of values and expressed its disgust through the most diverse means, ranging from rebellion, anarchy, and apocalypticism to aristocratic self-exile. So, more than its positive aspirations (which often have very little in common), what defines cultural modernity is its outright rejection of bourgeois modernity, its consuming negative passion." He also states, "However, on a much larger social plane, today's 'pop hedonism,' cult of instant joy, fun morality, and the generalized confusion between self-realization and simple self-gratification, has its origin not in the culture of modernism but in capitalism as a system that, born from Protestant work ethic, could develop only by encouraging consumption, social mobility, and status seeking, that is, by negating its own transcendental moral justification." (7).

6 Ibid. (5).

7 Tafuri, in discussing the state of the twentieth-century capitalist metropolis, states, "Of course, chaos is a datum and order an objective: it is sought within it. It is order that confers significance upon chaos and transforms it into value, into 'Liberty.'" Manfredo Tafuri, **Architecture and Utopia: Design and Capitalist Development** (Cambridge, MA, 1976), 96.

8 Fifty percent of telephone numbers in California are unlisted: Pacific Bell 1991.

9 "Capitalist development must negotiate a knife edge between preserving the values of past commitments made at a particular point in time, or devaluing them to open up fresh room for accumulation. Capitalism perpetually strives, therefore, to create a social and physical landscape in its own image and requisite to its own needs at a particular point in time, only just as certainly to undermine, disrupt and even destroy that landscape at a later point in time. The inner contradictions of capitalism are expressed in the restless formation and reformation of geographical landscapes. This is the tune to which the historical geography of capitalism must dance without cease." D. Harvey, **The Urbanization of Capital** (Baltimore, 1985), 150.

10 "The superimposed layers of the recombinant image share the similar 'thinness' of Duchamp's infrathin. These layers exist in a collapsed (discontinuous) space time, that unstable plane where disparate elements are forced to coexist. Phenomenally, this collapse results in the compression of experience." Central Office of Architecture, **Recombinant Images in Los Angeles** (Los Angeles 1989).

11 Jean Baudrillard writes: "The proliferation of technical gadgetry inside the house, beneath it, around it, like drips in an intensive care ward, the TV, stereo, and video which provide communication with the beyond, the car (or cars) that connect one up to that great shoppers' funeral parlour, the supermarket, and lastly, the wife and children, as glowing symptoms of success...everything here testifies to death having found its own ideal home." See Jean Baudrillard, **America** (New York, 1990).

In addition. Paul Virilio states: "Where once the polis inaugurated a political theatre, with its agora and its forum, now there is only a cathode-ray screen, where the shadows and specters of a community dance amid their processes of the disappearance of urbanism, the last image of and urbanism without urbanity. This is where tact and contact give way to televisual impact." See Paul Virilio. **Lost Dimension** (New York, 1991).

12 Carlo Aymonino states: "The character ( or meaning ) of a city is related to the degree of overlaying of spatial and interpretive elements, to the point in which they become indispensable to each other. This indispensability may only result in a 'judgement' if one reinterprets each time all the elements in the game; and to reinterpret means to plan...from this view point, the problems of 'insertion' and the more generic one of the 'environment' do not exist any more. What remains is the problem of more or less  formally completed architectural complexes and urban sectors." Carlo Aymonino. "L'edificio e L' ambiente: premesse alla progettazione." lectures at the Corso di composizione dell' IUAV (Venezia, 1967). 20-21 of the proofs.

13 "The airplane is the product of close selection
The lesson of the airplane lies in the logic which governed the statement of the problem and its realization.
The problem of the house has not yet been stated.
Machinery contains in itself the factor of economy, which makes for selection.
The house is a machine for living in."
Le Corbusier. **Towards a New Architecture** (New York, . 1960 ed.). 100.

14 "The house, the street, the town, are points to which human energy is directed: they  should be ordered, otherwise they counteract the fundamental principles round which we revolve; if they are not ordered, they oppose themselves to us, they thwart us, as the nature all around us thwarts us, though we have striven with it, and with it begin each day a new struggle." Le Corbusier. **City of To-morrow and Its Planning** (New York, 1929). 15.

15 Foucault states: "Order is, at one and the same time, that which is given in things as their inner law , the hidden network that determines the way they confront one another, and also that which has no existence except in the grid created by a glance, an examination, a language; and it is only in the blank spaces of this grid that order manifests itself in depth as though already there, waiting in silence for the moment of its expression." Michel Foucault. **The Order of Things: An Archaeology of the Human Sciences** (London, 1966).

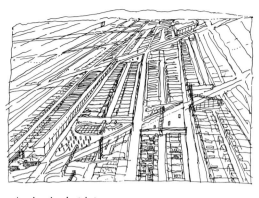

Los Angeles: Aerial view
of site intervention and
environs

Central Office of Architecture

Vicinity

While many spectacular building sites exist in Los Angeles, most of the land is characterized by unremarkable conditions. Large zones are devoid of any perceivable geographical features thus encouraging the repetition of a simple unsophisticated house type ad infinitum.

The site for this project is a nearly flat block bounded on all four sides by different conditions. To the south is Washington Boulevard, a commercially zoned street which becomes a major thoroughfare during peak commute hours. Hauser Avenue, on the west, is a well-used secondary street traveled by motorists trying to avoid the parallel-traffic-clogged primary streets. On the east is Ridgeley Avenue which terminates at the north end of the site where it is crossed by the Ballona Creek. Once a natural creek, the Ballona Creek is now a concrete walled flood control channel but still retains the intrinsic value of an identifiable geographical feature.

Re: American Dream

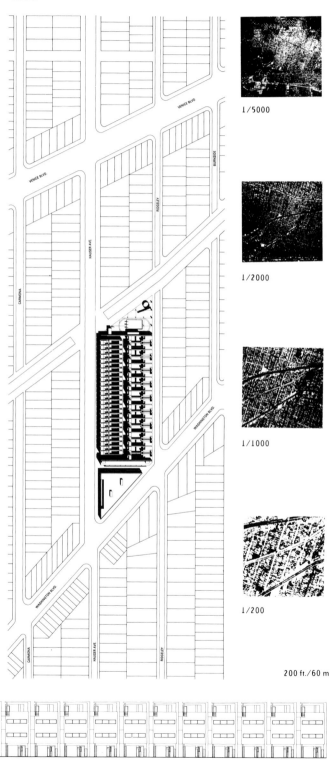

1/5000

1/2000

1/1000

1/200

200 ft./60 m

Hauser Facade

20 ft./6 m

Site Plan

Figure 1: Current division of property ownership.

Figure 2: Reduction of lot size reduces land cost per dwelling.

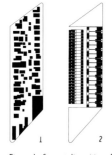

Figure 1: Current disposition of dwellings results in wasted outdoor space.

Figure 2: Buildings are located at the perimeter of the site, maximizing usable outdoor space in the form of courtyards and clearly defining the street edge.

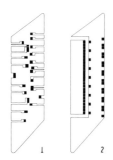

Figure 1: Current location of garages and consequential waste of land for driveways.

Figure 2: All garages and carports are linked directly to streets and alleys.

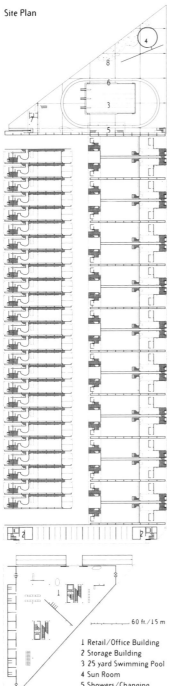

60 ft./15 m

1 Retail/Office Building
2 Storage Building
3 25 yard Swimming Pool
4 Sun Room
5 Showers/Changing
6 Running Track
7 Lifeguard/Security
8 Orchard

The block is divided in two parts by an alley. On Hauser twenty-two-feet-wide lots replace the existing fifty-feet-wide lots. This narrow width is a minimum which will allow for two side-by-side parking spaces. On Ridgeley the lots are thirty-three feet wide. A retail/office building is proposed at the south end of the block on Washington and a storage building forms an interface between this building and the housing units. As a consequence of the increased density, a new park has been created at the north end of the block next to the creek.

The objective of accommodating higher density housing than now exists in the area was accomplished by reducing the lot sizes and extending the building volume upwards. Individual land ownership is preserved while doubling the existing number of houses. In order to maintain privacy under this increased density, a system of high walls separates the lots.

The reduction of lot size is compensated by the efficient reallocation of outdoor space. The great amount of land previously devoted to front and side yards and driveways has been internalized and made useful.

Reduction of the building footprints allows the placement of additional units along the alley.

Central Office of Architecture

Ridgeley Facade

20 ft./6 m

The solution combines
three different units each
of varying size and each
responding to its location
within the block. The living
area of each type of unit is
located on a different level
to minimize unwanted
views into neighboring
units.

## Hauser Unit
**Lot size: 22' x 108'**
**three bedrooms**
The forty foot height of these
units is a response to heavily used
nature of Hauser Avenue. The
height yields two benefits: the
protection of the interior of the
block and the reinforcement of
a strong street edge. These lots are
accessible from both ends. Cars
must park in the garage off the
alley, above which an additional
room is located, while pedestrians
may enter from Hauser. The living
space is on the first floor and is
open to the courtyard and the
master bedroom is on top.

## Ridgeley Unit
**Lot size: 33' x 80'**
**two bedrooms**
Ridgeley Avenue is a relatively
quiet street due to the Ballona
Creek which crosses at the north
end and bars through traffic.
Units on Ridgeley are lower in
total height but still provide an
interior double height space as do
all the units. Entry is through a
small court on Ridgeley and the
living space, which occupies the
ground floor, maximizes openness
to the courtyard. The bedrooms
are located above on the first
floor.

## Alley Unit
**Lot size: 33' x 42'**
**one bedroom**
These vertically organized units
are distributed along the Ridgeley
side of the alley. Garages are
shared by paired units. Pedestrian
access from the street is maintained by way of an elevated
semi-private walkway. The living
space is a double-height volume at
the top connected to a sleeping
porch by an exterior stair. A bedroom is provided below the living
area.

Ground Floor Plans

Hauser Unit

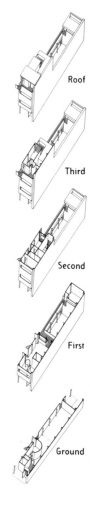

Roof

Third

Second

First

Ground

Ridgeley Unit

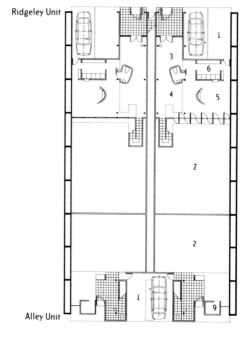

Alley Unit

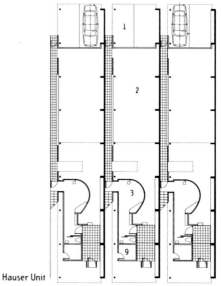

Hauser Unit

1 Garage
2 Courtyard
3 Entry
4 Living
5 Dining
6 Kitchen
7 Bedroom
8 Bathroom
9 Storage

10 ft./3 m

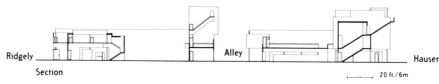

Ridgely

Alley

Hauser

Section

20 ft./6m

Structure, infrastructure, and circulation are planned to achieve efficiencies made possible by the transformation to higher density. With regularization of the house plans come economies in providing the required services. Points of connection can be reduced in number.

A system of walls containing the water, gas and electrical services while also providing structural support crosses the site. Alternating with these walls are rows of columns which raise the units and liberate the ground.

The courtyard and the columned space beneath the units provide for different types of outdoor activity. The courtyard is a private contained space removed from the chaotic condition of the city.

Ridgeley
First Floor

Alley

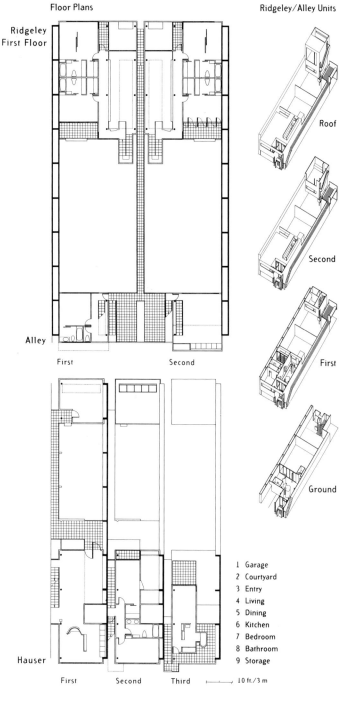

First     Second

Roof

Second

First

Ground

Hauser

First     Second     Third     |——→ 10 ft./3 m

1 Garage
2 Courtyard
3 Entry
4 Living
5 Dining
6 Kitchen
7 Bedroom
8 Bathroom
9 Storage

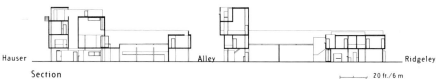

Hauser     Alley     Ridgeley

Section                    |——→ 20 ft./6 m

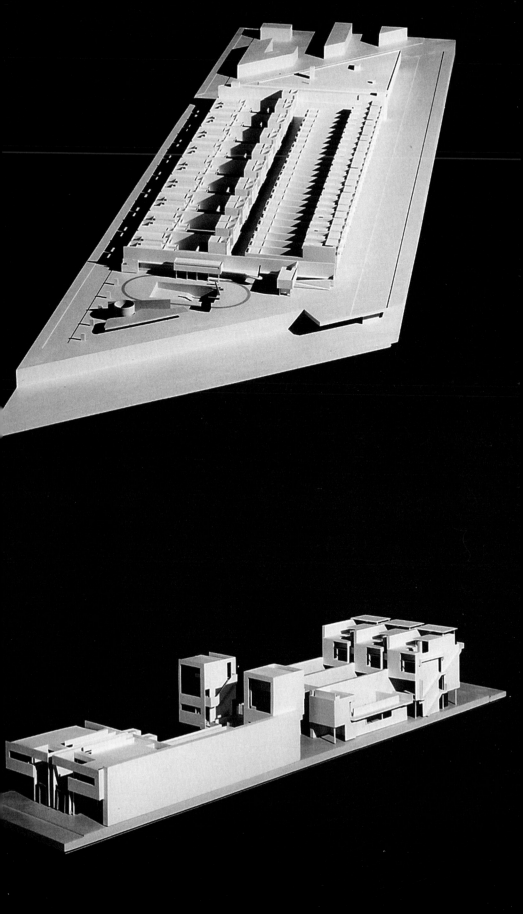

# Steve Johnson  James Favaro

## Pursuit of Happiness

Re: American Dream

**I**n Los Angeles middle-class families live in detached houses next to other middle-class families, independents live together in tracts of apartment buildings, and the wealthy live in pockets of high-profile seclusion like Bel-Air. In a city striated by large R-1, R-3, and R-15 zones, the social benefits of interaction across economic boundaries are not produced spontaneously or informally. There is no "sharing of the wealth." As much as the materially poor might live vicariously through the display of the wealth of others, the spiritually poor might benefit by contact with those for whom the pursuit of material riches has (either by necessity or by choice) assumed a lower priority.

The diversified zoning code puts people of all economic strata in proximity with one another. The fine-grained system of through-block streets provides open public spaces where people of all walks of life are able to encounter one another on a daily basis, and where children can play, young adults congregate, and the elderly participate in real life. The expenditures of the wealthy benefit all, for not only does the wealthy person build a wall of her house but she provides a wall for a public space beyond the boundary for her house. In this small way material wealth takes on a social significance.

The diversified zoning code makes an architecture which looks diverse because it is diverse in a socially authentic way, with variety which is not the result of artificially prescriptive laws such as complex setback formulas or material or "style" requirements. The result is more dynamic democratic urban form in which economic status is neither looked down upon nor excessively revered.

### Sensitive Dependence on Initial Conditions
The diversified zoning code establishes a framework for a future order without dictating a priori the physical form. As an open-ended plan it is sensitive to fluctuating economic climates and evolving demographics. Unit-density quotas for properties in each quarter-square-mile district provide the initial conditions for development but quotas are filled according to demand on a first-come-first-serve basis. How an individual property is developed is dependent on a variety of conditions such as the allowable unit-density, the willingness of the owner to sell or develop, and the local economic climate including the states of the construction industry and the real estate market.

The shape that the building takes is dependent on the programmatic requirements of the individual developing the property and the surrounding context, both of which cannot be predicted by the general plan. The character of each increment provides the context for the next increment and so on in an unpredictable and still ordered way. Thus

as the plan is put into practice the conditions of its implementation are constantly changing.

The uniform height limitation and setback requirements provide for the overall unifying counterweight to the diversifying forces of the zoning law. The architecture of the city thus becomes unified yet varied, chronologically responsive—its form never final, yet dependent on the initial conditions of its development, unpredictable but rational, and spontaneous within a structured socially viable framework.

## Culture Lag

The domestic architecture of Los Angeles betrays the origins of its builders in places east of the Rockies, themselves culturally linked to northern Europe (England, Germany, and others)—hence the odd juxtaposition of the little wood house with its elm tree and green lawn (more at home in Ohio) against the overwhelming background of stark mountains, parched landscapes, and big sky.

The new architecture of Los Angeles will take shape in concert with emerging new ways of living, compatible with the climate here and the pragmatic realities of a large metropolitan center. This combination of the overriding natural features and the characteristically American land subdivision system which defines the character of Los Angeles's infrastructure together with the social climate generated by the entertainment and high-tech industries provides clues to the emerging soul of the city and the kind of architecture which will eventually arise as a reflection of it.

Our plan codifies this new architecture and provides for an orderly process of its realization: abundant sunlight means that outdoor spaces can be tall and narrow and still be light—outdoor places need to be shaded to stay cool and here buildings or walls are better than trees because trees need water. Gardens can be enclosed and sparse with oak and lupine and granite floors instead of the elm and the rose and grass. The front lawn will disappear and outdoor living will take place in big rooms without roofs. Tall walls will shade long narrow streets, stairs will carry you to swimming pools and solariums on the roof and the picture window will move up the wall and onto the ceiling (as a skylight, or open-air roof aperture) to open out to the brilliant blue sky.

Johnson Favaro

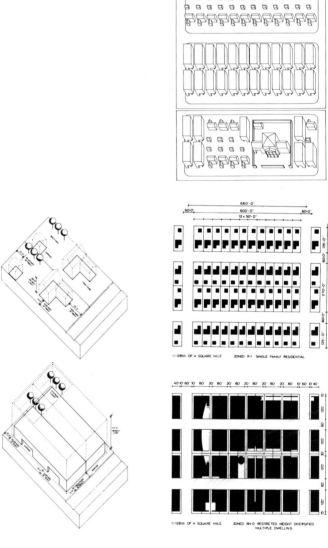

1/128th OF A SQUARE MILE     ZONED R-1  SINGLE FAMILY RESIDENTIAL

1/128th OF A SQUARE MILE     ZONED RH-D  RESTRICTED HEIGHT DIVERSIFIED
                                          MULTIPLE DWELLING

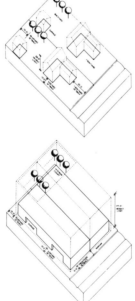

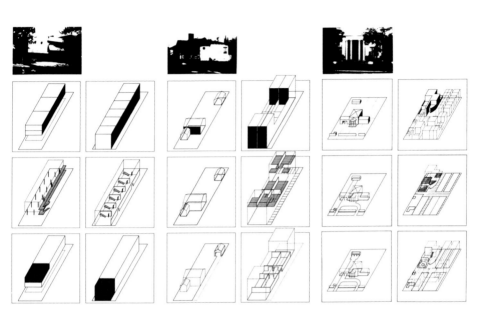

Johnson Favaro

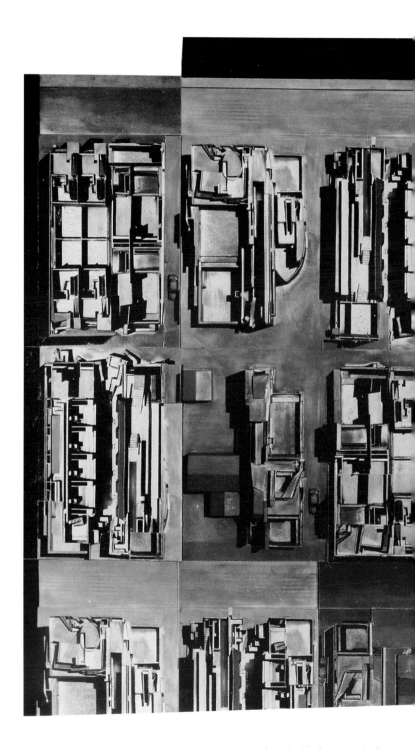

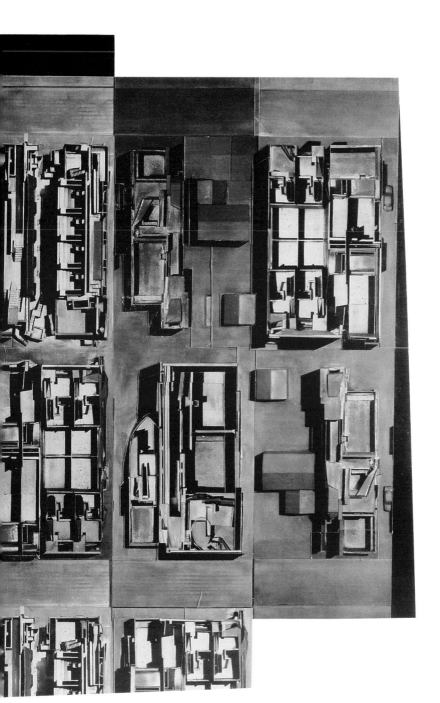

Johnson Favaro

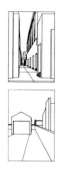

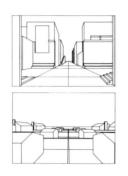

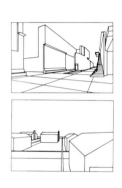

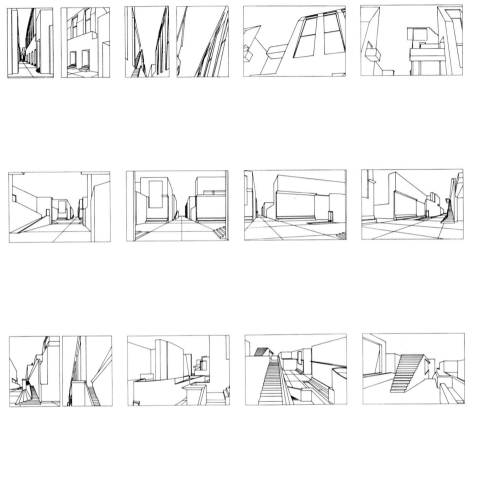

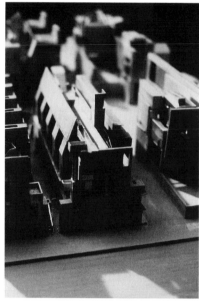

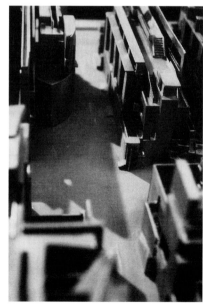

Johnson Favaro

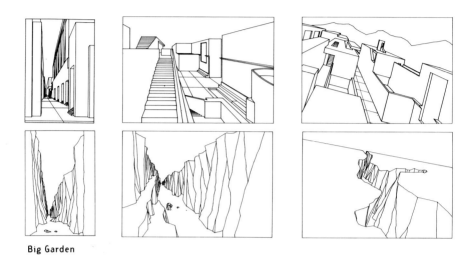

Big Garden

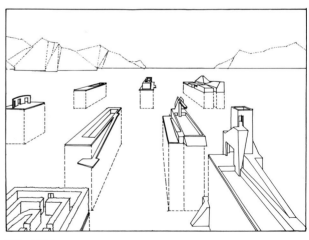

Picture This

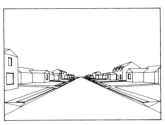

Grass and Trees

Real Land Reform

What a View

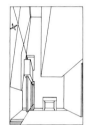

Picture Window

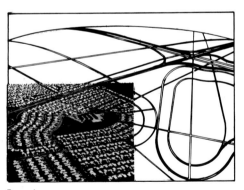

Enough

City of Los Angeles
Areas Zoned R-1

# Guthrie + Buresh

Team: Danelle Guthrie, Tom Buresh, Stefan Hellwig, Thomas Stallman, Steven Spier,

Neal Freedman-Borsuk, Maria Arroyo, Ingalill Wahlroos, Robert Keller, Jonathan Davis.

Re: American Dream

This proposition, re: housing in Los Angeles, begins with the observation, analysis, and manipulation of the existing conditions of the city. This response acknowledges a space and use between the purely suburban and the historically urban, a space and use that is between the private and the public. This is a site-specific architectural solution that will allow the incremental re-occupation of a particular neighborhood. Implicit in this thesis is the recognition and acceptance of the archetypal American desire for a freestanding single-family dwelling, although the hardships endured to sustain this dream, be they measured by money or time of commute, are well documented and evident.

We believe the existing fabric of the city to be potentially meaningful. The scale and position of the existing house, the given dimensions of the lot, and the cadence of the block are therefore viable permanences upon which this project is founded. This leads us to accept such formal conditions as the street as the primary public space, the imagined opacity of the property line, the house as an individualized object, the necessity of private, open space, the psychological importance of the lawn, the small scale and simple construction technology of a house, the predominant horizontality of Los Angeles, and the perceptual dominance of the sky.

This project analyzes a specific neighborhood, focusing on its available space, its uses, and its density. The site's natural boundaries are La Brea Boulevard and Fairfax Boulevard to the east and west, and Melrose Avenue and Beverly Boulevard to the north and south. These streets border the site with a ring of heavy commercial use. The area within them is peculiarly pedestrian oriented for Los Angeles; it hosts hip stylishness and retail on Melrose and Orthodox Jewish synagogues nearer Beverly, both of whose subcultures walk along the streets, though separately and for separate purposes. Between these two boundaries lies a 1930s-era tract of small, freestanding, single-family houses.

Within this portion of Los Angeles the apparent homogeneity of the tract development belies several distinctive spatial and usage types. We propose to heighten these distinctions by manipulating the current typology of the streets. Through observation of the site we propose three new street types: Hybrid, Private, and Open.

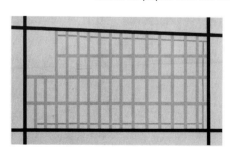

Existing Street Zoning

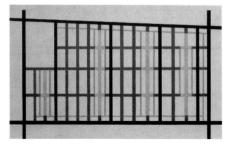

Proposed Street Zoning

Existing Figure/Ground

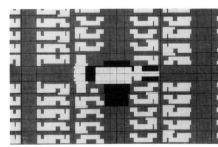

Proposed Figure/Ground

Guthrie + Buresh

# Hybrid Street

These are currently thoroughfares lined with existing houses behind a front-yard setback. In response to the heavy automobile use of these streets and the reality of the many people who now work in their homes, we propose adding small-scale

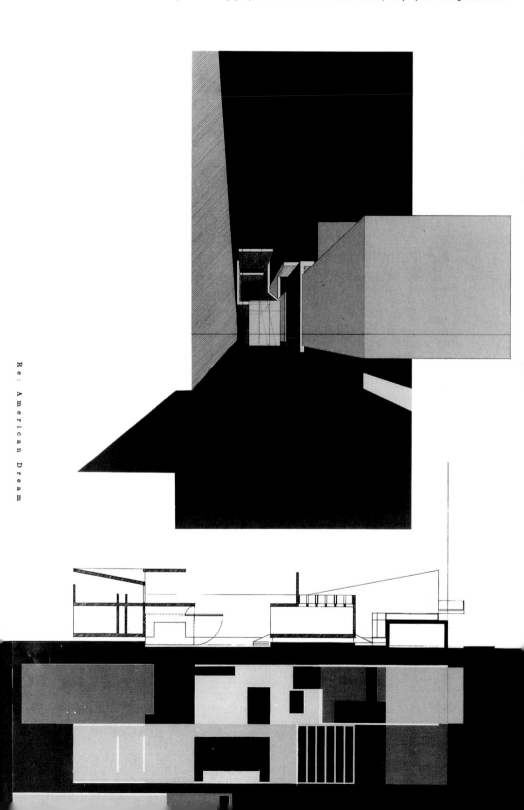

offices and studios at the front property line, with housing leaning out over them. The studios will serve as visual, aural, and zoning buffers between the residential units and the street.

Guthrie + Buresh

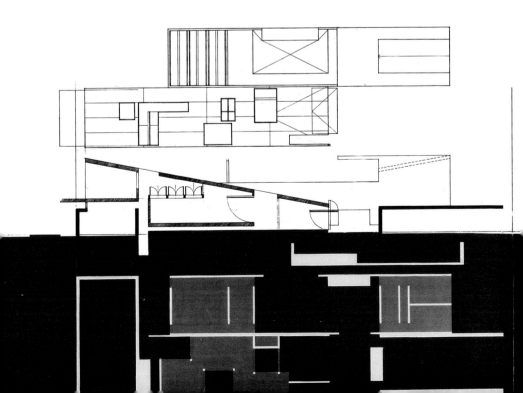

**Private Street** This is an access street inserted as an easement through the existing rear yards. Fronting it will be smaller-scale houses and garages. With the creation of these streets the existing lots can be subdivided crosswise and lengthwise, creating enough room for two separate units where previously there was one, plus an additional unit between the lot lines. This will eliminate the need for a driveway cutting through

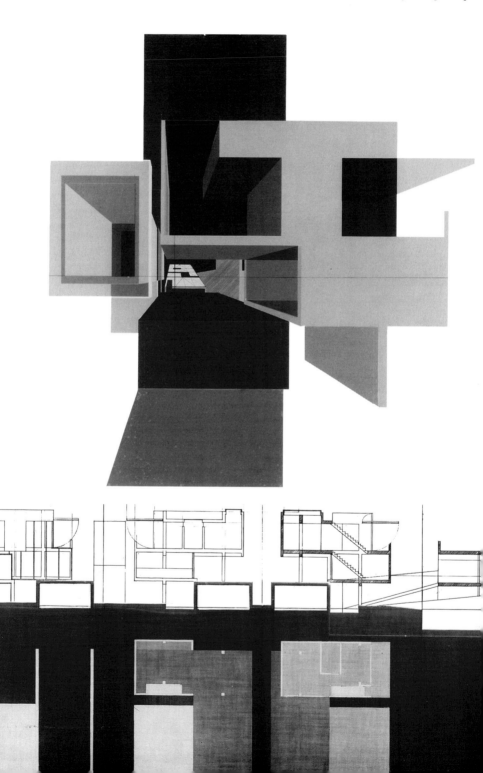

the yard to a freestanding garage in the rear. The existing garage will be demolished. The new houses, due to their proximity and the need for privacy, will have to respond to each other formally in terms of mass, void, and openings. They will strive for autonomy with minimal means. Within this configuration a required percentage of private open space would be preserved for each house, in addition to some shared outdoor space.

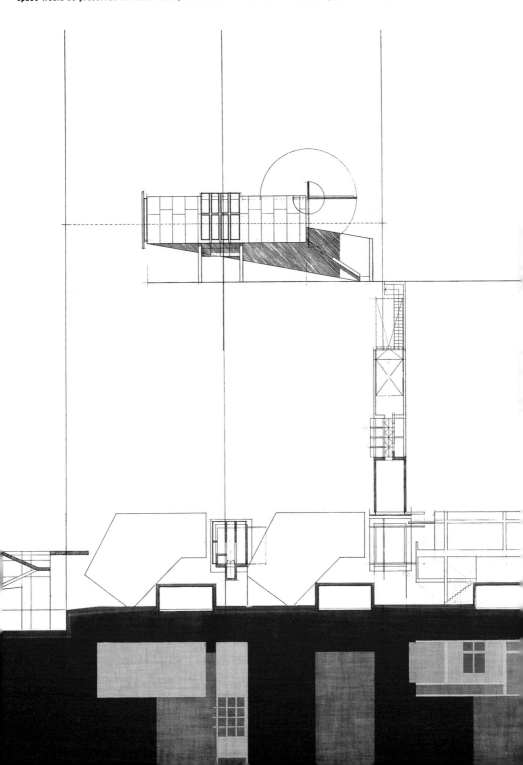

# Open Street

Replacing a lightly traveled street will be a common green space interspersed into the new pattern. Programmatically it will function as open space for the neighborhood, though formally it will be both figure and ground. Inserted into these open streets will be multiple housing or shared community functions in opposition to and criti-

cal of the predominately isolationist preoccupations of the existing populace. These buildings will be places of refuge, both programmatically and spatially, with their monumentality tempered as they crouch near the ground.

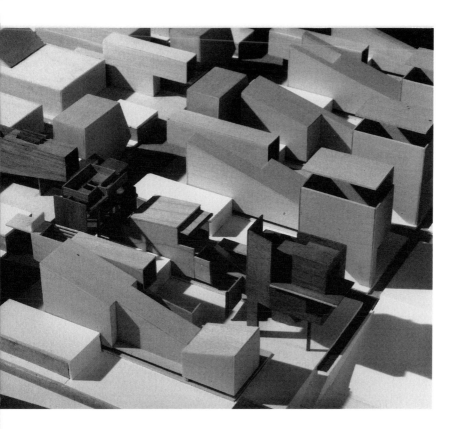

Guthrie + Buresh

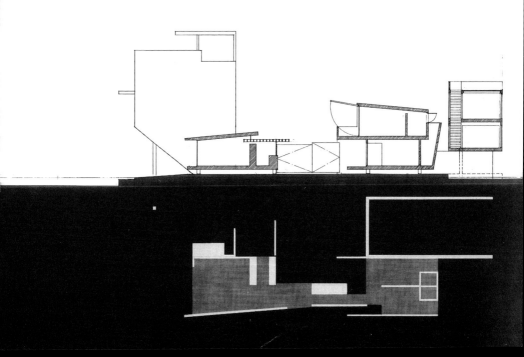

# Incremental Growth

1. Existing lot with single-family house and garage.
2. Introduction of private street and new garage at the rear and an office/studio space in the front yard setback.
3. Positioning of a new house in either the rear yard, partially over the garage or in the side yard, both fronting the private street.
4. Erasure of the existing single family house and creation of two autonomous houses. Private exterior space is provided within the envelope of each house, semi-public exterior space occurs on top of the garage. Through-block pedestrian access is maintained to the public space located at the Open Street.
5. Fully realized development from Hybrid Street to Open Street.

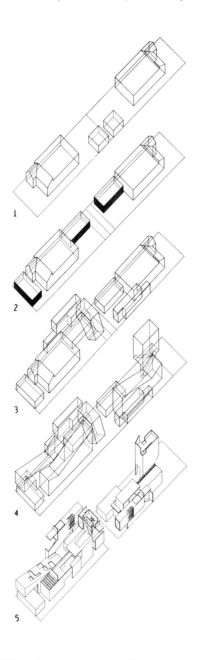

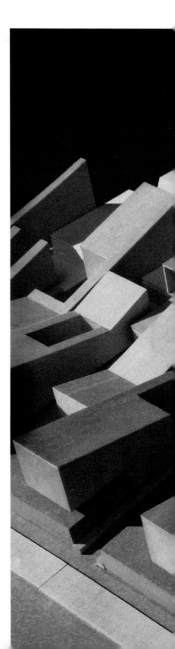

## Object/Field Blur

Within this hierarchical overlay of distinctive street types we propose an object/field blur composed of streets, buildings, space, and their occupation. At differing scales we propose a constant shift between the elements of the composition: at the scale of the city, the streets comprise the dominant figural element against the ground of the blocks; at the scale of the block, the buildings-as-objects compose a field; and at the scale of the buildings, the exterior space foregrounds as the buildings recede. A dense and pressurized composition is created through an intentional, and in some cases confrontational, overlapping of enclosed private spaces, semi-private exterior spaces, and the public spaces of the Open Street.

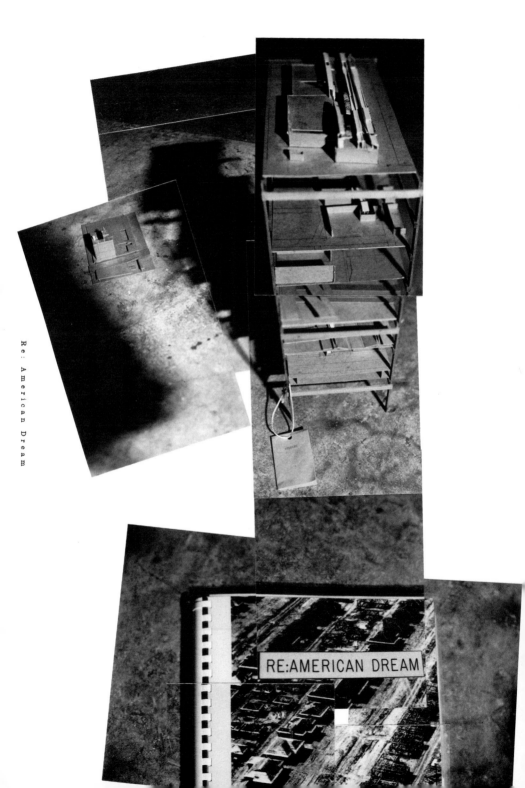

RE:AMERICAN DREAM

# Mary-Ann Ray

This project attempts to build houses that will not alter or disrupt the existing structure of the city, but which will be layered on top of and between the existing structure. This project will not replace, substitute, reorganize, rehabilitate, or redo the form or elements of the existing city. Instead, it will investigate possibilities for insertion, add-on, attachment, inclusion, inlay, and superimposition.

This project will attempt to provide houses for those ways of life present in 1990s Los Angeles that are unaccommodated by existing houses. The size, scale, organization, location, and cost of existing houses are fixed, predictable, and in proliferation. Density, transcience, single people, extended families, and minimum-wage earners are left out of the existing formula. This project attempts to "build in" to the structure of Los Angeles the pluralism that exists.

This project works toward a densification of the city. Densification is seen as a positive thing—it makes houses for those who want them, and allows undeveloped land outside the city to remain undeveloped. Densification may allow the city to become more labyrinthine at times, while more clear and crystalline at other times.

This project will attempt to find and make use of land or sites presently available but unused. Many of these sites will raise questions about the importance and necessity of land ownership. All of the houses in this project detach themselves from the ground and turn toward the sky. The lawn on the land is here a planted plane facing the sky.

Finally, this project will attempt to make houses which explore a lightness and economy of construction, one that is more temporary and portable than that found in the American or southern California single-family house.

Team: Felix Ang. Angela Brooks Scarpa. Annie Coggan. Darlene Crosby. Michael Gruber. Timothy Higgins. Bijoy Jain. Nicholas Lowie. Carol Lowry. Elizabeth Martin. Kenny Sizemore

Mary-Ann Ray

The Street House occupies a thin piece of land beside a city street, over a city sidewalk, beside a large parking lot. It occupies the public land of the city, never crossing over to touch down on private lots. The Street House will be set amongst active street life. There are shared showers and bathrooms near ground level, a big public room up high under big rafters, and places to get food and mail on the ground level. There are many single rooms in the Street House, each opening to an exterior entrance stoop and stair (there is no internal circulation in the Street House). The rooms are designed less as walls and floors and more as parts of furniture—bed, chair, table-top, desk. The fabrication of the walls and roof trusses

The Street House makes a house for people who live on the street now without a house.

will take place in adjacent parking lots by the people who may live there. The walls are constructed of reused wood, and are assembled in a patchwork-like manner. The walls of the Street House will be raised during a kind of public celebration by means of ropes, pulleys, and cranes. The construction of the Street House will make a kind of urban drama.

The **Park House** uses as its site the tops of existing parking garages in the city. The long thin rows of the Park House sit above the parking so that very few spaces are lost. The Park House will make streets and gardens and lawns suspended above the top of the city. The Park House will make the most out of living high in the sky—seperate from the ground plane of the city, while at the same time within walking distance of it.

**The Park House makes a house for people who come and go and who do not wish to settle in one place forever.**

The **Long House** will run across the ground plane of the city—finding space between buildings, over streets, and across large fields of parking lots. There will be many places made for living inside the Long House. Each place to live will be reached by its own stair—there are no running corridors or balconies in the Long House. Because of this, light and air enter the house from both sides. Each place to live will have a lawn and a room to the sky on the roof. There will be places made for the city beside and under the Long House—parking courtyards, newstands, etc. The Long House will be like a horizon or a direction encountered in the existing pattern of the city. It will be surfaced with a luminous color so that it will change throughout the day—reflecting the color of the light and sky.

**The Long House makes a compact and affordable house for people who are workers in the city, and for loners.**

The **High House** will use the vacant top floors and roofs of existing buildings as sites. The High House will attempt to make the occupation of the upper reaches of the host building spectacular. Wooden ramps, stairs, rooms, roof parts, light wells, and gardens/lawns will rise above and drop below the roof plane of the host building. They will populate the space of the top floor and make a new landscape on the roof. The High House dweller is not asked to be a landowner. There is no land to own in this house that sits between a floating plane and the sky.

**The High House makes a house for people who live and work in their house above the city.**

The **Many-Family House** densifies the lot of the single-family house through the addition of a moveable house. The placement of the moveable house in the backyard will form a courtyard with the existing walls of garage, fence, alley, and non-moveable house. The moveable Many-Family House is made of wood, and the wall structure is a kind of hollow diaphragm. Cabinetry and parts of rooms can occupy the space within the diaphragm at certain points. The Many-Family House can be independent and self-sufficient, or the larger kitchen and facilities of the existing single-family house may be shared amongst the inhabitors of the lots.

The Many-Family House makes a house for people who wish to live near to other people, but who may someday move on.

## Bibliography

Italo Calvino, Invisible Cities, trans. Will Weaver (New York, 1978).

J.B. Jackson, "The Westward Moving House," and "Stone and its Substitutes," in Discovering the Vernacular Landscape (New Haven, 1984).

Gwendolyn Wright, "Family Patterns," in Building the Dream: The Social History of Housing in America (New York, 1981).

Mary-Ann Ray

Street House

## Street House

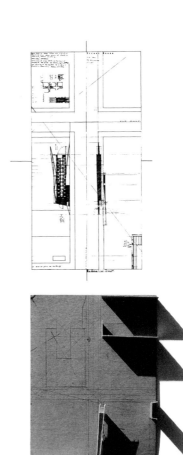

Mary-Ann Ray

# Park House

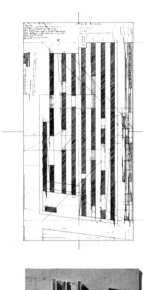

Mary-Ann Ray

# High House

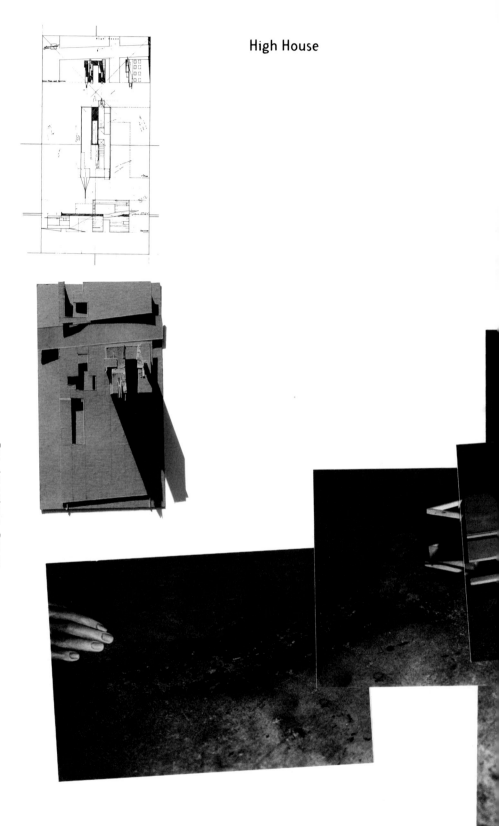

Mary - Ann Ray

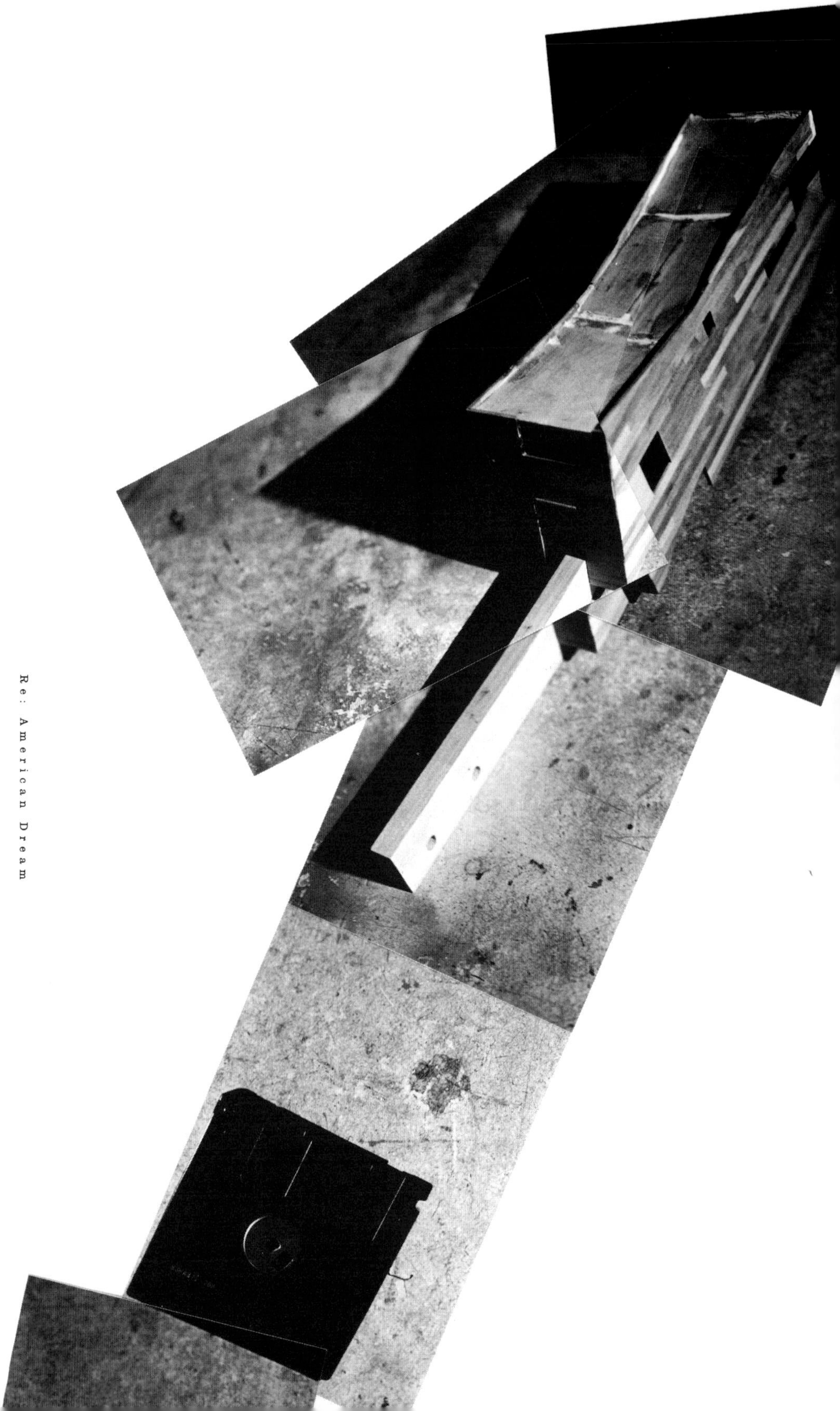

Re: American Dream

# Many-Family House

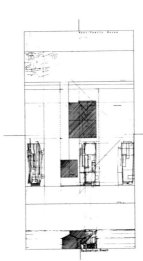

# Roger **Sherman**

Team: Douglas J. Giesey, Lisa Towning, Nicholas Louie, Michael Prentiss, Mehmet Kürükcuoğlu

Re: American Dream

**We propose to turn the single-family residence in Los Angeles inside out.**

This project treats the house as a landscape around which the familiar amenities of suburban living are organized and upon which the scenes of domestic life may daily be played out. In doing so, we seek not to dismantle but rather to amplify the conventions of suburbia, and the contemporary obsession with individual privacy which it represents: that is, the desire of the resident to remain anonymous, to retreat from public view, and to seek both refuge and a stage for self-expression within the protective envelope of his or her own private property/precinct.

In addition, our proposal considers two other critical concerns which the inherited model of the single-family detached house fails to address. The compact arrangement of interior living spaces within a single volume renders the tract home poorly suited to the mild southern California climate, which affords the opportunity to establish the yard as an integral extension of the spaces within the house itself. Like the dwelling type indigenous to this region, the adobe (fig. 1), and house forms in other regions of similar climatology (fig. 2), our project envisions the suburban yard as the center of domestic life, as acting in the capacity of an outdoor living room.

**1** Baldwin Ranch Adobe. Los Angeles. c. 1900

The detached home is also deficient with respect to the changing socioeconomic and demographic climate in Los Angeles, which suggests a desperate need for smaller houses on less land, more efficiently utilized. Our project demonstrates that by eliminating the outmoded zoning setback requirement and allowing the house to be organized around its yard area rather than in the midst of it (figs. 3, 4), residential property can be better utilized. With an increasingly large percentage of the cost of a single-family residence comprised by its land value—a cost which escalates everyday—this project reduces the dream of the suburban home to its essentials and makes

**2** House of the Vetii. Pompeii. c. 1st century

### 3 Zoning Envelope

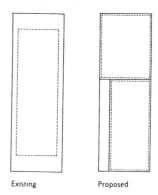

Existing        Proposed

it affordable to more of those who desire it.

      This proposal is designed to densify the residential fabric of the city incrementally—one property at a time—by empowering individual homeowners to develop their own properties. It calls for a change in current zoning legislation in order to permit Los Angeles's ubiquitous 50-by-150-foot lots to be subdivided into two smaller (front and rear) subparcels of equal size (fig. 5). Automobile access would be provided to the rear property via a drive along the side of the front parcel. The proceeds from the sale of one of the subparcels would in turn enable the existing homeowner/ developer to finance the construction of a new house on the remaining subparcel (or sell both subparcels and move elsewhere). This would represent the logical and final extension of the very development process by which the land in and around the Los Angeles Basin has been subdivided continuously over the roughly 135 years that have elapsed since the first (Ord) survey was drawn of the original pueblo settlement. In that time, the Los Angeles metropolitan area has witnessed the successive subdivision of land into tracts of progressively smaller size (fig. 6).

      Along the newly redrawn lot lines, a network of partywalls would be erected which formalizes the ad hoc use of various types and combinations of walls and planting (fig. 7) to demarcate property boundaries. Each existing lot would be developed as either the right or left hand of a matching couple, pairing the driveways and the walls which enclose them to create a single interstitial, semiprivate court for the common use of the adjacent four units. Elsewhere, the partywalls lend necessary uniformity to the street frontage, privacy to the residents within, and an improved scale to the narrowed space of the street (fig. 8).

      Inside the walls is installed an alphabet of spatial characters, each of which corresponds to the suburban-scaled yard of an individual residence (fig. 9). These

Roger Sherman

### 4 Disposition of Rooms

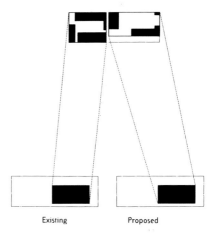

Existing        Proposed

### 5 Figure/Ground

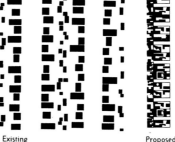

Existing        Proposed

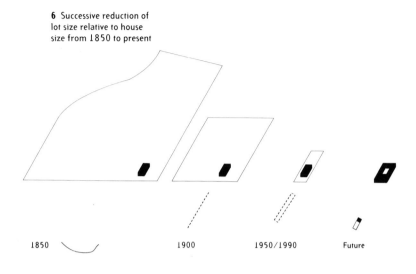

**6** Successive reduction of lot size relative to house size from 1850 to present

1850          1900          1950/1990          Future

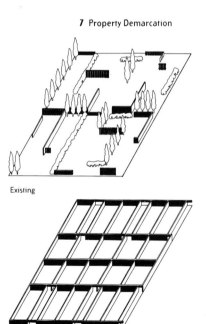

**7** Property Demarcation

Existing

Proposed

figured spaces, whose arrangement within any particular block is a consequence of individual choices made by each homeowner, are employed as a means of establishing a heterogeneous system by which to identify and differentiate one residence from another (figs. 10, 11). In order and configuration, the shape of each character is incidental to the programmatic anatomy of the dwelling. They are intended to simultaneously expose the superficial methods of differentiation promoted by builders' stylistic assignations and acknowledge the somewhat more genuine differences created through customization of those dwelling types by homeowners themselves (fig. 12, 13, 14).

At the scale of the individual residence, each of these courtyard spaces is itself further differentiated in satisfying its own unique and complex set of programmatic demands. These are answered by two principle means: first, through the variegated patterning of materials, textures, and changes in ground plane (figs. 17, 18); and second, in being populated with an assortment of thematic elements commonly associated with, and significant of, residential life: the hearth/fireplace, hearth/entertainment center, antenna, porch, laundry line, and shade tree (figs. 15, 16, 19). Each surface or element serves in turn to "furnish" the otherwise neutral spatial figure of the yard. Other important amenities of suburban living provided within each dwelling include: the ability of the automobile to enter and be stored within each separate property; the yard; the possession by each house of its own entrance; the psychological separation between any residence and the the properties it adjoins; and the provision for private, clandestine relationships to be formed between neighbors (figs. 20, 21).

The houses are layered in such a way as to metaphorically relate each to its larger natural, domestic, and urban context (fig. 22). The first is evident by the presence in each house of a below-grade excavation for storage of perishable goods; the second represented in the living level of each dwelling, where activities relating to family take place within the confines of an enclosed outdoor space; and the last by the roof level, which affords expansive views across the landscape of residential rooftops to the horizon, and offers places both to rest and to exercise under the sheltering sky. The experience of such varied landscapes from within each house makes each a true microcosm of the experience of Los Angeles itself, a city of layered existences.

Roger Sherman

**8** Streetscape

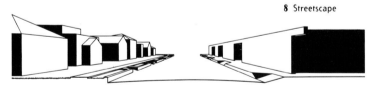

Existing                                                   Proposed

**9** Residential Characters

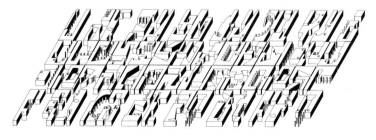

11 Model overview showing
hypothetical arrangement
of residential characters
intermingled with single-
family homes.

10 Figure/ground drawing
depicts proposal fully developed

Re: American Dream

Existing                                    Proposed

**12** Typology & Difference

**13** Plan of residential block. showing solid (black) and void. domestic features

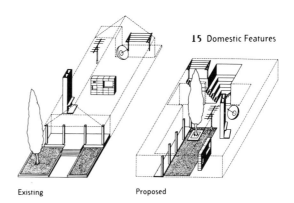

**15** Domestic Features

Existing          Proposed

**14** Figure/ground plan (detail)

Roger Sherman

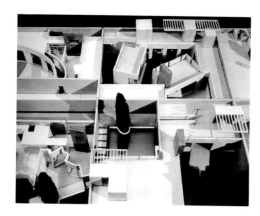

**16** Model, transverse
overhead view

**17** Plan of residential
block arrangement of
exterior ground surfaces/
patterns/ textures

**19** Model, detail overview
showing domestic elements

**18** Detail plan of exterior
ground surfaces

Roger Sherman

**20, 21** Plan view of model
showing four sub-parcels
grouped about common
drive courts

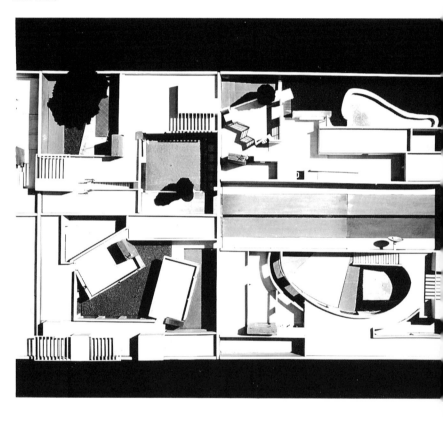

**22** Model. transverse view
showing partywall divisions

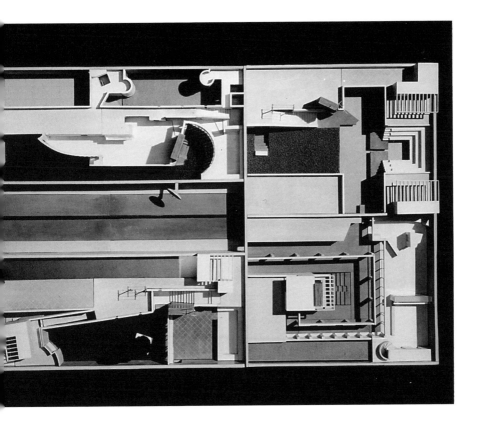

Roger Sherman

Sylvia Lavin received her doctorate from Columbia University's Department of Art and Archaeology in 1990. An assistant professor of architectural history and theory at UCLA and frequent guest critic at SCI-Arc and USC, she has written and lectured extensively on the work of Gehry, Venturi, Graves, Predock, and other contemporary architects. As a historian, she focuses on architectural theories of the eighteenth century and is the author of **Quatremere de Quincy and the Invention of a Modern Language of Architecture** (Cambridge, MA, 1992).

John Kaliski is Principal Architect of the Community Redevelopment Agency of the city of Los Angeles where he oversees urban design policies, architectural review, historic preservation, and the design and planning review policies of the agency's citywide housing and citywide childcare programs. A graduate of Yale University where he received his B.A. and M. Arch. degrees, he worked as a designer for Skidmore, Owings and Merrill, taught at the University of Houston College of Architecture, and now teaches design studios and urban theory seminars a SCI-Arc. His numerous writings have appeared in **Cite, L.A. Architect, Texas Architect**, and other publications.

Janek Bielski received his B.A. from the University of Southern California, his graduate diploma from the Architectural Association School of Architecture in London, and is a licensed architect in the state of California. His work has been published in **A · U, L'Arca, L'architecture D'Aujourd'Hui, Archithese, Sites**, and **Progressive Architecture**. He was awarded the 1990 Young Architect Award from the Architectural League of New York and was a finalist in the 1987 International Design Competition for the West Hollywood Civic Center. He is a frequent guest critic at SCI-Arc, UCLA, and USC.

COA is comprised of Ron Golan, Eric A. Kahn, and Russell N. Thomsen, all of whom received their Bachelors of Architecture from California Polytechnic S.L.O. in 1981. Golan received his M. Arch. from SCI-Arc in 1986. Their office, established in 1986, works on both built and theoretical work, as well as teaches architectural design studio at SCI-Arc. They have lectured in Los Angeles and New York; completed projects and theoretical urban proposals for Los Angeles have been exhibited and published in the United States, Europe, and Japan.

Steve Johnson, who has taught as a design instructor in both the graduate and undergraduate programs at SCI-Arc, received his B. Arch. from the University of Florida in 1979 and his M. Arch. from Harvard in 1983. James B. Favaro graduated Phi Beta Kappa from Stanford University's School of Engineering in 1978 and then received his M. Arch. from Harvard in 1982. A recipient of the 1985 Rome Prize, he has taught at UCLA, USC, and RISD. In 1988, he established a private practice in partnership with Steve Johnson.

Danelle Guthrie and Tom J. Buresh established the firm Guthrie · Buresh Architecture in 1988. Ms. Guthrie received her B.A. in Architecture in 1981 from UC Berkeley, and her M. Arch. in 1985 from UCLA. Mr. Buresh received his B.A. in Architecture in 1978 from Iowa State University, and his M. Arch. in 1985 from UCLA. He is a member of the faculty in the Graduate Program at Sci-Arc. Their work has been published in **Kenchiku Bunka**, the **UCLA Architectural Journal, Offramp, Violated Perfection, Experimental Architecture in Los Angeles**, and **Now Time**.

Mary-Ann Ray teaches architecture at SCI-Arc. She has a B.F.A. in painting from the University of Washington in 1981, an M. Arch. from Princeton University in 1986, and was a Rome Prize Fellow for 1987-1988. Currently, she practices with Robert Mangurian at Studio Works, Venice, California and at Atelier Italia, Ronciglione, Italy.

Roger Sherman received his B.A. from the University of Pennsylvania in 1980 and his M. Arch. from Harvard's Graduate School of Design in 1985, and maintains an architectural practice in Los Angeles. He was a recipient of the Harvard University Wheelwright Traveling Fellowship in 1992, and winner of the West Hollywood Civic Center International Design Competition of 1987. His work has been published in **Architectural Review** (U.K.), **Progressive Architecture, Architectural Record**, and the **Los Angeles Times**. Mr. Sherman is a studio and seminar instructor at SCI-Arc and UCLA.

Jennifer Schab, educated at Rhode Island School of Design and Columbia University, is a practicing architect in Los Angeles and instructor at the Otis Institute of Art and Design.